THE CRISIS OF THE GERMAN LEFT

Monographs in German History

THE CRISIS OF THE GERMAN LEFT

The PDS, Stalinism and the Global Economy

Peter Thompson

Berghahn Books
New York • Oxford

Published in 2005 by

Berghahn Books

www.berghahnbooks.com

Library of Congress Cataloging-in-Publication Data

Thompson, Peter, 1960 July 22-
  The crisis of the German left : PDS, Stalinism and the global economy /
Peter Thompson.
    p. cm. -- (Monographs in German history ; v. 13)
  Includes bibliographical references and index.
  ISBN 1-57181-543-0
    1. Parties des Demokratischen Sozialismus (Germany) 2. Germany--Politics
and government--1990- 3. Communism--Germany (East)--History. 4. Germany--
Economic conditions--1990- 5. Germany--Social conditions--1990-6.
Globalization. I. Title. II. Series.

JN3971. A98P3779 2004
324.243'027--dc22

                                                              200405384
British Library Cataloguing in Publication Data

A catalogue record for this book is available from the British Library.

Printed in the United States on acid-free paper

ISBN 1-57181-543-0 (Hardback)

CONTENTS

PREFACE AND ACKNOWLEDGEMENTS

I would like to acknowledge the kindness and support of many individuals and institutions without whom this book would not have been possible. Firstly I would like to thank all of my colleagues at the University of Sheffield – as well as the university itself – for supporting the study leave without which it would be impossible to undertake any extended research activity. Professor Moray McGowan was a great help in encouraging me to undertake this work and in supporting me throughout his time at Sheffield. Professor Michael Perraudin continued that role when he assumed the Chair of German at that university. I would also like to thank Professor Alan Bance and Dr Peter Barker for their helpful comments on early drafts of this work. I would also like to thank Reiner Oschmann, the former Pressesprecher of the PDS parliamentary party, for his enthusiastic support during my research trips to Berlin and Gregor Gysi, André Brie and Yvonne-Sylvia Kaufmann for granting me interviews which helped to further my understanding of both the party and the wider society.

Most of all I thank Dr Karen Leeder for her love, encouragement and tireless – and very necessary – proofreading and corrections as well as the intellectual stimulation which she always provides. I also thank Paschal Sheeran for his friendship and support through the years. Finally, I thank Günter Minnerup for his help in getting me into the academic business in the first place and for the support and intellectual inspiration he has provided since. I owe him a great debt of thanks.

I dedicate this book to my children: David, Philip and Rosa.

LIST OF ABBREVIATIONS

CDU   Christlich Demokratische Union
COCOM Coordinating Committee for Export to Communist Areas
COMECON   Council for Mutual Economic Assistance
CPSU   Communist Party of the Soviet Union
CSU   Christlich Soziale Union
DVU   Deutsche Volks Union
FAZ   Frankfurter Allgemeine Zeitung
FDP   Freie Demokratische Partei
FRG   Federal Republic of Germany
GATT   General Agreement on Tarrifs and Trade
GDP   Gross Domestic Product
GDR   German Democratic Republic
GNP   Gross National Product
IMF   International Monetary Fund
KPD   Kommunistische Partei Deutschlands
KPF   Kommunistische Plattform
MF   Marxistisches Forum
NAFTA   North American Free Trade Area
NATO   North Atlantic Treaty Organisation
NÖSPL   Neues Ökonomisches System der Planung und Leitung
NSDAP   Nationalsozialistische Deutsche Arbeiterpartei
PDS   Partei des Demokratischen Sozialismus
SBZ   Sowjetische Besatzungszone
SDP   Sozial Demokratische Partei (GDR)
SED   Sozialistische Einheitspartei Deutschlands
SMAD   Sowjetische Militäradministration in Deutschland
SPD   Sozialdemokratische Partei Deutschlands
SZO   Soviet Zone of Occupation
USSR   Union of Soviet Socialist Republics
WTC   World Trade Centre
WTO   World Trade Organisation
UPDS   Unabhängige Partei des Demokratischen Sozialismus

INTRODUCTION

While waiting on the tarmac in East Berlin for the arrival of Mikhail Gorbachov on his fateful visit of the summer of 1989, Erich Honecker responded to the journalists' shouted questions about the future of the GDR by saying that 'reports of its death have been much exaggerated'.[1] Within 16 months the state had disappeared and along with it the SED, its ruling Communist Party. In the months after the fall of the Berlin Wall the SED underwent a period of convulsion and transformation which saw the expulsion of many of its old hard-line leaders and their replacement with more moderate and reformist forces from within its own ranks. There was a move towards a more pluralistic socialist outlook, an end to the dogmatic approach of the Stalinist system and, above all, a gradual – though reluctant – acceptance that Germany would be united and that the ex-Communists would have only a minor role to play in that new nation. In December 1989 the SED mutated into the SED/PDS and then, in February 1990, into the PDS. For most commentators, the days of both the state and the party, in whatever form, were numbered. The first and last free parliamentary elections in the GDR on 18 March 1990 brought in a governing coalition of centre-right forces under the premiership of the CDU leader, Lothar de Maizière, committed to the reunification of Germany.

What the collapse of the GDR has left behind, however, is a greater sense of East German identity than probably ever existed before 1989 and a continuing political presence for the PDS which has confounded many commentators and dismayed many of its political competitors. Even though at the time of writing this introduction, the fortunes of the PDS are not at their highest point, there is every reason to believe that situation could change again, just as it did in the mid-1990s.[2] The reasons for this are manifold and reside in complicated social and psychological

1. 'Die totgesagten leben länger'.
2. See Dan Hough, *The Fall and Rise of the PDS in Eastern Germany*, Birmingham, 2002, for a discussion of the varying fortunes of the PDS.

factors to do with the reciprocal relationship between the need for both individual freedom and social security in the ex-GDR. As Tanja Busse and Tobias Dürr have pointed out recently, many of the facets of eastern German identity are very similar to those of immigrant communities arriving in a new land. Without having physically moved, East Germans have indeed come to a new country and, like all immigrant communities, they have brought with them their own world-views and values and their own political cultures.[3] This includes continuing, though perhaps unstable, support for the political party most identified with the ex-GDR, namely, the PDS. The continuing obsession with the GDR and growing self-identification as East German rather than just German also parallel the continuing and even growing identification which many third-generation immigrants in West Germany have with their grandparents' homelands. This is unlikely to fade in the near future and may indeed last for many decades. After all, 300 years after the Act of Union in the U.K. there would appear to be little decline in the national identity of the Scottish people, despite attempts to create a British identity. Before 1989 it used to be said that there were two states in one German nation; now it could be argued that there are two German nations in one state.

However, the PDS finds itself in a situation in which it is only reluctantly a regional party and, indeed, wishes to see itself as an increasingly all-German socialist, left-social democratic or even Marxist party, able to mobilise opposition to the growing political, social and economic dislocation engendered by the marketisation of the German economy. The extent to which it will be able to play this latter role is under discussion here. There is little sign of it at present and indeed, recent elections have seen it in steady decline in its heartlands in East Germany as well. However, Germany is really only just beginning to enter a process of reform and economic adjustment which Britain undertook some thirty years ago, with the advent of monetarism under a previous Labour administration and its entrenchment under Mrs Thatcher. The political consequences of the neo-liberal undermining of the Rhenish capitalist model which, until recently, was accepted by almost all parts of the mainstream political spectrum in Germany have yet to be fully felt. It is for this reason that it would be too early to write off the PDS completely, despite the very real difficulties which it is at present experiencing.

The aim of this study is to help towards an understanding of the very complicated development of identity and opinion in the ex-GDR since 1990 in its proper historical and theoretical context. The first two-thirds of this book look at the long waves and trends at work in the socio-economic development of twentieth-century Germany. This represents an attempt to separate out the structural and the conjunctural factors at play in global politics and to identify which is most important at specific

---

3. Toralf Staud 'Ossis sind Türken', *Die Zeit* no. 41, 1 October 2003, p. 9

historical and political moments. The main part of the analysis discusses the shift from the primacy of politics, which prevailed throughout most of the twentieth century, to the primacy of economics, which has prevailed from around the middle of the 1970s and is the basis for what is widely known as globalisation but which is essentially about the creation of a market-state in which finance capital and neo-liberal short-termism has replaced the productivist imperative. The impact this shift had on the workers' movement in both East and West is obvious and yet incompletely understood, not least because the ideological shift which has accompanied the economic one has been so complete that what used to be seen as relatively moderate demands, such as the social imperative behind even Christian Democratic programmes, are now seen as dangerously radical and yet at the same time a part of the 'forces of conservatism'.

This book is not an exhaustive or empirical account of the fortunes of the PDS as a contemporary political party. There are many such studies and simply to add to them would not be of great benefit. Instead, this book sets out the development of the 'Stalinisation' of the communist movement in Germany in the context of a global primacy of politics. It discusses the role and function of the SED in the GDR and the continuing debate about the extent to which the PDS is simply the successor party to the SED and therefore irretrievably 'Stalinist' as is often maintained also within this global political context. The main question though, is the extent to which it is a new departure from its own past, able to jump over its own shadow.

In 1944 Karl Polanyi, in his book *The Great Transformation*, argued that the rise of fascism and the Second World War had been brought about by the shifting balance in the relationship between politics and economics in the first part of the twentieth century.[4] He believed that the ascendance of market liberalism and the primacy of economics had brought about a dislocation which issued directly into social instability. In many ways, what I have tried to do here is to adapt this analysis to the collapse of communism and to see the latter as a symptom of the re-emergence of a triumphant market neo-liberalism out of the economic crisis of the 1970s which continues to reshape the world. In that sense this book is about the second great transformation, this time at the end of the twentieth century, and the effect that it is having on the world in general and Eastern Germany in particular.

When looking at Eastern Germany and the PDS we can see that the history of the GDR and the SED has both uses and disadvantages for the PDS and that the monumentalist, antiquarian and critical elements at work in the history of the German workers' movement continue to function both positively and negatively within the party. In an interview conducted in 1998, the then Deputy Chair of the PDS, Sylvia-Yvonne

4. Karl Polanyi, *The Great Transformation*, Boston, 2001.

Kaufmann, spoke of the 'rucksack of history'[5] which the party is obliged to carry with it. This was meant as a metaphor for the burden of the GDR past, but a rucksack is also a very useful thing to carry on a journey. What this book aims to do is to unpack the PDS's rucksack and find out what is in it. To what extent are its contents weighing the party down and impeding its progress, and to what extent are they useful on a journey which is taking Germany through a second great transformation?

The PDS arouses passions on all sides, which remain to a large extent irreconcilable. It is what makes it one of the most interesting parties to study in Europe today, but it is also what makes it one of the most difficult to fully comprehend. Above all, this is because to understand the party today it is necessary to grapple with some of the fundamental dilemmas of twentieth-century political life as it relates to the German workers' movement. As Gerhard Schürer stated in his evidence to the Enquête-Kommission on the history of the GDR and the role of the SED:

> If one analyses the power structures [of the GDR], then one must also study their relationship to the Soviet model which was adopted. One has to analyse the history of both East and West Germany. One has to analyse the Cold War. I don't think one can say that one does not have space or time for it. On the contrary, it is essential to any convincing historical analysis of the GDR.[6]

In order to understand the PDS, therefore, one has to understand the SED and the GDR. But in order to understand them one has to understand the relationship between Stalinism and the Cold War. However, these phenomena only become clear if, in turn, one has a grasp of the fundamental turning-points in the history of the twentieth century, and the motivating forces behind them. The relevance of this historical framework will become clear during the exposition of the themes contained here.

In any perusal of the books and pamphlets on the PDS, from both within its own ranks and outside, one is struck by the omnipresence of the historical debate and the lessons which that history can teach. On the one hand the party is attacked for still believing in 'socialism' in a post-socialist world. On the other hand, those within the party understand socialism in very disparate and vague terms. Furthermore, the Stalinism debate within the party, which has consumed much theoretical energy in since 1989, has produced relatively little enlightenment but has at least allowed the different factions to present their own political credentials.

What all of those factions have in common – no matter how far apart they may seem – is their commitment to a sense of the primacy of the political and the collective over the individual and the purely economic.

---

5. Interview with Yvonne Kaufmann, Karl Liebknecht Haus, 26 September 1998.
6. Gerhard Schürer was a member of the Politburo of the SED from 1973 to 1989. See *Getrennte Vergangenheit, gemeinsame Zukunft*, 4 vols, Munich, 1997, vol. 1, pp. 50–51.

The main difference arises not over whether the approach should be a collectivist one, but where the locus of collectivism should rest: with the community or with the state. Since 1990 the party has had to try to maintain its position as representative and defender of the community of the ex-GDR, whilst at the same time attempting to become a party with a role to play at the federal state level. The PDS has reached that point which faces all those parties which start off as anti-systemic: namely, whether to criticise the system or to exercise power within it, or indeed both. The latest developments and the outcome of the city elections in Berlin in 2001, in which the PDS gained nearly 50 per cent of the votes in the eastern parts of the city, and the federal election of 2002 in which it maintained a high level of support in the East but still failed to leap the 5 per cent hurdle would seem to suggest that the party has begun to turn back towards its own community in the ex-GDR for support. It is attempting to solve or at least ameliorate the dilemma of power by exercising it in the East as a form of opposition to the prevailing Western-dominated federal system.[7]

This dichotomy is compounded by the fact that in the East it has to appeal to voters who are, in traditional political terms, relatively conservative whilst trying to appeal to radicalised and marginalised groups in the West. Paradoxically, therefore, its association with the GDR and the SED is not an expression of its political radicalism but of its social conservatism and is of considerable benefit to it in the ex-GDR. In the West this social conservatism can be a deterrent to winning over the libertarian Left, who traditionally vote Green. Concepts such as order, discipline, family, community and nation do not have the same negative connotations in the East as they do for the Western Left. It is certainly the case that within the PDS there is a tendency towards the acceptance of traditional hierarchical categories. As Toralf Staud has pointed out, the values of the membership of the PDS tend to be quite conservative compared with those of the Western Left, and the election in October 2000 of Gabrielle Zimmer as the new leader, to replace Lothar Bisky, seemed to imply a retreat by the party into its heartlands.[8] This was compounded by the federal election defeat of 2002 and the fact that, despite that defeat, Zimmer was re-elected as party leader. Zimmer stepped down, however, in June 2003 and Bisky took over once again as party chairman. He saw part of his job, and was supported by Zimmer in this as well, as attempting a reform of the party's fundamental positions and the adoption of a 'basic programme' which moved the party increasingly away from its more orthodox traditions towards a modernised socialism,

7. At the time of writing, in addition to its acquisition of governmental responsibility in Berlin, it was in government in Mecklenburg-Vorpommern and supported the red-green government in Sachsen-Anhalt and the SPD minority government in Brandenburg as well as forming the governing party in many cities and local authorities.
8. Toralf Staud, 'Auf dem Weg zur CSU des Ostens', *Die Zeit* no. 43, 19 October 2000, p. 6.

capable of accepting important changes to the structure of the global economy and supporting the 'enterprise culture' as something positive.

Within the Gysi/Bisky/Brie group the trend has long been to try to break out of the traditionalist ghetto and turn towards a more liberal or even libertarian version of socialism that would appeal to Western voters. In the Berlin city election of 2001, Gregor Gysi was very much at pains to distance himself from the more orthodox views of his party in order to appeal to West Berlin voters. He stated, for example, that, in a conflict of interests between the party and Berlin, he would always choose Berlin. This is a radically liberal position for any party leader to take and is even more the case in a party which emerged out of the rigid democratic centralism of the SED.

In general, then, we can say that the PDS continues to represent a part of the Left historically anchored in collectivist values but with increasingly libertarian tendencies which are bound, one might say designed, to upset the more traditionalist wings. The struggle for the direction and locus of the party is far from over. Put in general terms, the East/West split is compounded by the Left/Right split but the outcome of these constant splits and fusions will be determined by forces and developments beyond the party's control. As Yvonne Kaufmann has maintained, 'The PDS is a party opposed to the prevailing system. That is central to the identity of the party. Without it we would be superfluous.'[9] Its whole political physiognomy is an expression of a commitment to socialism in its traditional vein but with modernising influences. Effectively it wishes to return to being a pre-Stalinist communist party, with a Marxist base but a lively culture of factions, tendencies and discussion but with one important dimension, namely that of revolution, largely removed. Despite the replacement of Zimmer with Bisky and a more liberal orientation, the PDS will remain a party of the East and that it will be forced to be anti-systemic within its electoral fortress of the ex-GDR rather than the whole of the Federal Republic. This demonstrates that the basic values of the PDS, although still of the Left, are actually fundamentally different from those in the West. Its 1968 was primarily that of the Prague Spring rather than Paris and it did not grow up in the context of the Anglo-Saxon individualism which so characterises the mainstream Western liberal Left. For this reason its roots are in a more orthodox Marxism, tempered by a regionalist nationalism, in which values of order and community take precedence over individualism. Whether there can be local solutions to global problems today remains, however, an unanswered question. And when we look at that question in the context of the notion of the end of ideology which claims that there can no longer be global solutions to local problems, we can see the nature of the crisis which faces the PDS and the Left in general.

9. Interview with Yvonne Kaufmann.

However, what worries the leadership of the PDS is not so much the need to maintain a Marxist focus: Yvonne Kaufmann maintains that the party is proud to see itself as part of a tradition stretching from Marx and Engels via Liebknecht and Luxemburg.[10] However it is also concerned that for anti-PDS commentators of the Centre and Right, but also for the more orthodox members of the party in the Kommunistische Plattform (KPF) and the Marxistisches Forum (MF), there is, in effect, little or no difference between Marxism and Stalinism. A recent example is to be found in an essay by Konrad Weiss, where Marxism is equated with Stalinism in a very black and white view of the PDS: 'I believe that a Saul can become a Paul; the Bible describes that quite clearly. But I do not believe in mass conversion as a result of a conference resolution: a resolution which makes Marxists into democrats, militarists into pacifists, militant atheists into believers, privileged functionaries into lovers of humanity.'[11] The end result is that both of these elements supply each other with ammunition for their cause. The Right can point to the existence of the KPF and MF and maintain that the party is therefore still 'Stalinist' and the KPF and MF can point to the fact that the leadership has talked about their expulsion as proof that the party is in danger of becoming 'social-democratised'.[12] An almost obsessive discussion of Stalinism and the Stalinist nature of the GDR is therefore central to the electoral fortunes of the party, rather than, as some see it, a harmful diversion from the reality of day-to-day politics. The real locus of the problem lies not in the theoretical hair-splitting but in the fact that any attempt to prioritise the political over the economic is therefore seen as essentially dogmatic and therefore – in a Marxist party, at least – Stalinist.

The PDS is therefore confronted with the task of remaining a distinctive party of the Left in Germany (which means that it has to remain true to its roots in Marxism) and yet not appear so radical as to preclude the chances of cooperation at local and federal state level with parties which have long since arrived in the Federal Republic. As Michael Schumann observes: 'On the one hand there are those who solemnly celebrate their views of orthodox socialism in a sort of self-constructed religious fervour, whilst others – apparently far removed from all programmatic discussions and theories – carry out basic day-to-day policies.'[13] In other words, it is a party like any other. In order to survive in post-unification Germany,

10. Interview with Yvonne Kaufmann. See also the PDS Statute in both its 1991 and 1997 versions: http://www.pds-online.de/partei/dokumente/statut/.
11. *MUT, Forum für Kultur, Politik und Geschichte*. August 1998, http://www.bln.de/k.weiss/tx_total.htm
12. See Günter Minnerup, 'The PDS and Strategic Dilemmas of the Left', in Peter Barker (ed.), *The Party of Democratic Socialism in Germany. Modern Post-Communism or Nostalgic Populism?*, Amsterdam and Atlanta, 1998, p. 218.
13. PDS Executive Committee member Michael Schumann, http://www.ddr-im-www.de/Aktuelles/Sonstiges/040200.htm.

the PDS has to adapt to the very values which are so distant from its own traditions and at the same time try to bring its own values into the political agenda of the Federal Republic. It is in this context that the accusation of lingering Stalinist tendencies and social authoritarianism, which is often levelled at the party, has to be analysed. The aspects under examination are therefore not so much to do with the objective socio-economic but rather the subjective politico-cultural or even psycho-social situation in the ex-GDR since unification. However, one of the most important things to remember in any analysis of the debates within the PDS is, to paraphrase Karl Kraus, that even when it all appears to be about opinions and political positions, the determining contradictions exist in the real world and not merely in the heads of the participants.

Having said that, any conclusion reached on the PDS is inevitably determined by the political position of the observer. Patrick Moreau and Jürgen Lang, for example, see the PDS as a dangerous communist organisation, determined to reintroduce a Stalinist regime. [14] Equally Christian von Ditfurth sees it as a Trojan horse for the KPF and the MF: 'Bisky, Brie und Co. can get on with the business of presenting a modern, socialist face to the world. Uwe-Jens Heuer and his comrades are happy with that as long as they and the rest of their Marxist Forum can determine the central ideological basis of the party.' [15]

Eva Sturm, in the introduction to her work on the *Politikfähigkeit* (the acceptability or adaptability of a party to the mainstream) of the PDS, discusses the various ways in which parties in general and the PDS in particular are interpreted. [16] What emerges from her study is that the general attitude to any party on the part of most political scientists is based on the assumption that a party will not challenge the basic organisational tenets of the state. Any party which does so is automatically described as being politically *unfähig* (incapable or unacceptable). As we have seen above though, the PDS still understands itself, at least to some extent, as an anti-systemic party. Even if one rejects Patrick Moreau's very narrow definition of *Politikfähigkeit* as being merely about *Demokratiefähigkeit* in favour of a wider definition of it as one of exercising 'legitimational, representational, integrational, transmissive and indicative functions', as Sturm does, [17] this still leaves out of the equation the right and ability of a party to challenge the existing form of state and democracy.

As we can already see from these few examples, much of what is written about the PDS's position is designed to deny the PDS its own

14. Patrick Moreau and Jürgen P. Lang. *Linksextremismus. Eine unterschätzte Gefahr?*, Bonn, 1996.

15. Christian von Ditfurth, *Ostalgie oder linke Alternative. Meine Reise durch die PDS*, Cologne, 1998, p. 69.

16. Eva Sturm, *'Und der Zukunft zugewandt'? Eine Untersuchung zur 'Politfähigkeit' der PDS*, Opladen, 2000.

17. Ibid., p. 13.

political legitimacy and challenge its right to existence in the form that it sees fit. The party's continued existence and electoral prosperity have to be seen, therefore, not only in their contemporary but also in their ideological and its historical contexts. It is the uses and disadvantages of history for the PDS – the contents as well as the specific weight of the rucksack – which are under consideration here.

In the first two chapters the categories of monumental, antiquarian and critical history are borrowed from Nietzsche and applied to an analysis of the German workers' movement. Stalinism is defined and its development traced from high to neo-Stalinism. Stalinism itself, however, is in turn put in a firm historical, socio-economic and inter-systemic context. The twentieth century is broadly defined as a short political century driven by the need to integrate the working class into the social project and subordinate economic decision making to the political exigencies of the Long Cold War between East and West. I have coined the term Long Cold War here to describe the global situation prevailing between 1917 and 1990, from the Russian revolution to the unification of Germany. Within this framework I analyse the history of the workers' movement as divisible into three distinct periods:

1. The period of critical Marxism (1850s–1920s) in which a critique of society and history was undertaken from a position of fundamental and radical opposition.
2. The period of monumentalist Marxism (1920s–1950s) in which both social democracy and communism exercised real power under conditions of ideological struggle and the fight for political hegemony and in which their attitudes to history and ideas were based in hypostatised dogma. That is, the ideologies of Weimar social democracy and Soviet Stalinism became reified into Bernsteinian and Marxist-Leninist dogmas respectively.
3. The period of antiquarian Marxism (1950s–1989) in which socialism in East and West became de-ideologised. During this period there was a depoliticisation of power, an integration of the working class into conservative social settlements on both sides of the Wall and a bloc mentality in which stability rather than progress or change became the highest goal.

The third chapter will deal with the consequences of these developments for the PDS today. There I shall also discuss the extent to which it is possible for the Left to move on to a new period representing a return to the critical tradition out of which Marxism grew, rather than a repeat of the monumentalist or antiquarian dogma which Marxism became.

This study concerns itself with the PDS's own self-understanding in the context of the history of the ex-GDR. It also seeks to challenge the common assumption that its support is simply based on a politics of protest at the socio-economic consequences of German unification. There is a fundamental critique here of the position taken by many commentators that the party is likely to fade as a political force once German unity becomes more established. In most cases this is no more than an expression of desire rather than of objective analysis. I shall argue that the decline facing the PDS since the election of 2002 is not necessarily a long-term one and that it is too early to write it off – once again – as a serious contender.

The motivating theme behind this study is to plot and analyse change and flux in global conditions and how they affect Germany and its political developments. It is no coincidence that German unification took place at perhaps the second most important turning-point in the twentieth century since 1917, namely, 1989/90. Rather, it represents an essential element of the second great transformation of the world economy. The relationship between economic transition and the collapse of the political superstructure of social states in both East and West in the latter part of the twentieth century will form a central part of the analysis here. It is therefore important to look at the party's potential impact as a social defence organisation as well as political party for both East and West in the coming period and the extent to which it can influence and shape the wider society in terms of cultural and political developments.[18] The reason for doing this lies with one further little-noticed contradiction facing Germany in the twenty-first century, namely the conflict of priorities between the axes of economics and politics.

There is a further division of the history of the workers' movement and the industrial world in the twentieth century. In chapter 2 it will be divided into three periods. For reasons of space and relevance the first period will be briefly described rather than deeply analysed:

1. The period (1850s–1917) in which political decision making largely issued from economic requirements. The working class was effectively excluded from power or government and imperial expansion and world trade dominated the political agenda.
2. The period (1917–1974) in which integration of a large and politicised working class led to the relative subordination of purely economic factors to socio-political necessity.
3. The period (1974–present) in which social cohesion has once again taken second place to the primacy of economic decision making.

If these two forms of periodisation are examined it is clear that they are interwoven and that the ideological turns which exist within the world of political history can be seen to be concurrent with – both determined by and determining – shifts in economic conditions. Below, I shall first deal with the ideological periodisation of the politics of the workers'

---

18. Gesellschaftsanalyse und politische Bildung e.V. (ed.), *Zur Programmatik der Partei des Demokratischen Sozialismus. Ein Kommentar*, Berlin, 1997, p. 13.

movement before going on to deal with the underlying economic and social forces at work.

Rather than seeing this as a simple base and superstructure model, however, I have interwoven economic, political and ideological components at all points. This is therefore a study which places the PDS in the context of an understanding of the continuing contradictions of socio-economic formations in the modern world. The problems facing Germany as well as the PDS at present stem from the fact that the shift from political to economic primacy has necessarily been accompanied by the end of the certainties and simplicities of antiquarian thinking. This conjuncture has been misidentified elsewhere as the end of history and ideology,[19] but I hope to show here how it represents, in fact, the recommencing of history and the end of de-ideologisation.

The reason for the confusion in these matters rests on the fact that the majority of analyses recognise the existence of one or another of these factors and yet they rarely tie them in together, nor do they look for motivating forces. Thus the shift back to the primacy of economics is widely recognised by many economists, social commentators and journalists and yet its connection with the collapse of communism and the end of ideology is largely seen as coincidental. Equally, those who work primarily in the realm of ideas see the end of communism and ideology as events and processes unconnected to tectonic shifts in the world economy. A thoroughgoing de-linkage of influences and forces has taken place which, in Habermas's words, has rendered the world *unübersichtlich* (incomprehensible).[20] The result of this has largely been a celebration of incomprehensibility rather than an attempt to clarify the situation.

Ralf Dahrendorf – in a remarkably Marxist class analysis for a convinced liberal – has also addressed these issues. He briefly outlines the emergence of a new global class and economic system which could only re-emerge with the end of the Cold War and the rebirth of class war:

> 1989 was not the end of history or the final triumph of democracy and the free market. In fact the opposite could be said to be true. History, for so long boxed in by the miserable coexistence of the two blocs, which needed each other in order to prevent change and maintain control, began to get under way again. In that sense the threat to democracy and the market has become reality rather than empty shadow-boxing.[21]

19. Francis Fukuyama, *The End of History and the Last Man*, London and New York, 1992.
20. Jürgen Habermas, *Die Neue Unübersichtlichkeit. Kleine Politische Schriften*, Frankfurt,1985.
21. Ralf Dahrendorf, 'Die globale Klasse und die neue Ungleichheit', *Merkur, Deutsche Zeitschrift für euopäisches Denken*, Stuttgart, no. 11, 2000, pp. 1057–1068. It is remarkable how many old liberals are using (albeit very vulgar) Marxist analysis these days. Marion Dönhoff writes about the *deutsche Leitkultur* (the dominant culture of Germany) in the following terms: 'The globalisation of economics and finance is largely complete. The same is true of supranationalism in politics and in communication. Culture will follow.' *Die Zeit*, no. 9 November 2000, p. 4.

The final sentence of this quotation is the most important in the context of this study. The end of reified monumentalist and antiquarian thinking is an absolute precondition for the return of critical history and, as far as the PDS is concerned, radical action.

This study is therefore an attempt at restoring comprehensibility to the many concurrent but disjointed debates about contemporary society and places a consideration of the PDS and socialism in that context. I have tried to do this whilst at the same time being fully aware of my own motivating interests. These are shared with John Elster when he maintains that 'the goal of the social sciences is the liberation of man'.[22] The choice of subject here is therefore certainly politically motivated and the conclusions arrived at will also inevitably be at least coloured by the author's views; yet it is hoped that the requisite objectivity in considering the evidence will be maintained.

This study has relegated empirical analysis to the role of supporting evidence for a theoretical framework which goes far beyond any mere consideration of the electoral fortunes of a given party. There are already myriad empirical studies of the PDS and the Left in general.[23] There are also those which deal with relatively superficial questions of political acceptability and the supply of and demand for political parties in some sort of electoral market-place.[24]

However, to take in the ideas of Nietzsche again, history itself is open to interpretation and functionalisation. Whilst not wishing to adopt the radically subjective positionism of Nietzschean thought, I do wish to avoid the pitfalls of vulgar-Marxist objectivism as it was too often practised in the GDR itself. The best way to avoid going too far along either intellectual path, it seems, is to merge them both: that is, to maintain that there is a historic truth about certain events, trends and tendencies in human history but that people construct their own truths about those events, trends and tendencies, not all of which have equal value, but all of which need to be considered.

22. John Elster, *Logic and Society: Contradictions and Possible Worlds*, Chichester, 1978, p. 65.
23. See, for example, Hough, *The Fall and Rise of the PDS in Eastern Germany*; Birmingham, 2001; Bisky et al., *Die PDS-Herkunft und Selbstverständnis*, Berlin, 1996; *Chronik der PDS 1989-1997*, Berlin, 1998; *Der schwere Weg der Erneuerung – Von der SED zur PDS. Eine Dokumentation*, Berlin, 1990; von Ditfurth, *Ostalgie oder linke Alternative*; Andreas Herbst G. Stephan and J. Winckler, *Die SED. Geschichte – Organisation – Politik. Ein Handbuch*, Berlin, 1997; Patrick Moreau, *PDS. Anatomie einer postkommunistischen Partei*, Bonn, 1992; Patrick Moreau, *Was will die PDS?*, Berlin, 1994; Gero Neugebauer and Richard Stöss, *Die PDS. Geschichte. Organisation. Mitgliederstruktur*, Opladen, 1996. For further texts see also the Bibliography.
24. In any case, many of these detailed empirical and statistical studies often come up with conclusions of a level of banality such as; 'the probability of a vote for an extreme right or left-wing party increases with the degree to which the voter thinks of himself as right or left-wing.' Rudolf Günter Deinert, *Institutionsvertrauen, Demokratiezufriedenheit und Extremwahl. Ein Vergleich zwischen westdeutscher Rechts- und ostdeutscher PDS-Wahl*, St. Augustin, 1997, p. 135.

Essentially, this study represents an unapologetic attempt to restore a grand narrative to our historical and political considerations. The approach taken here is to look for connections and to see the historical object of analysis not merely as a deconstructed set of free-floating metaphors but as a related and interpenetrating series of events and their consequences. After all, to paraphrase Marx, parties make their own history but not just as they please.

Chapter 1

ON THE USES AND DISADVANTAGES OF HISTORY FOR THE PDS

Nietzsche often discussed the relationship between the root and branch of a tree. The image can also be applied to an understanding of the PDS as a branch of the German workers' movement which did not wither and die as many had expected and, indeed, hoped. In Nietzsche, the size and strength of a tree is in proportion to the size and strength of its roots. What shows reflects what is hidden, and the relationship between surface appearance and radical essence is a dialectical one. The roots need the branches as the branches need the roots and each influences the health of the other.

To extend the metaphor for the discussion here, the point at which the PDS emerges as a branch is also tied up with the historical growth of the tree. As Nietzsche points out, the critical historian knows 'each primary nature was, at some point, a secondary nature and that each victorious secondary nature again becomes a primary one'.[1] In other words, it is impossible to trace the precise moment of genesis of any historical development, as each stage emerges from the old to become the new. The new carries within it large elements of the old and yet also transcends them and transforms them into something else. This is not merely the negation of the negation but the sublimation of the sublimation, to marry both Marx and Nietzsche.

For Nietzsche there were three forms of historical analysis and implementation: the monumental, the antiquarian and the critical.[2] These three categories can help us to understand not only the history of Stalinist ideological and political strategy in Eastern Europe but also the three basic tendencies within the PDS and their respective attitudes towards current political developments. The pattern of social authoritarianism present in

1. Friedrich Nietzsche, *Werke und Briefe*, Munich, 2000 (CD-ROM), p. 3896.
2. Ibid.

the development of the German workers' movement can be traced here and the way in which this influences the social and political attitudes of the PDS and its voters can be demonstrated. This grouping of issues also helps us to understand the reasons for the emphasis on historical debate within the socialist movement as a whole.

Nietzsche recognised that, to command the present and build the future, it is necessary to control the past. Human society was doomed to live contextually. That is, we are the only species which has a capacity to live through history. Our whole approach to our lives is therefore historical. We constantly compare what we do and what we want with our experiences. Politically, therefore, to be human is to be constantly retrospective. However, the main point Nietzsche was making about this retrospection is that it is inevitably distorting, relative and contingent. As he put it: '"I did that" – says my memory. "I cannot have done that" – says my pride and sticks to its guns. In the end it is memory which surrenders.'[3] This quotation can be seen to be relevant to many of the various stages of German *Vergangenheitsbewältigung*[4] and is certainly often used to explain the way in which the Left deals with the history of the GDR. As we shall see later, it is also the main criticism levelled at the PDS.

Nietzsche contended that Germany was a nation more aware of its history than most and that the need to create retrospective identification was correspondingly high. As Klaus von Dohnanyi puts it: 'we Germans go about analysing our history far more thoroughly than others, but then we have more reason to do so'.[5] Again, an understanding of the development of the workers' movement in twentieth-century Germany has to take account of the functionalisation and distortion of history which lay at the core of Stalinism. I shall attempt below to explain Nietzsche's three categories and indicate how they can be applied to the German workers' movement. This will provide the background to an attempt to unravel the genesis and development of Stalinism in Germany and look at its implementation as the functional basis of the GDR as a state. I shall then go on to analyse whether the existence of Stalinism for so long within the workers' movement has poisoned the tree beyond recovery. An alternative conclusion arrived at by the more traditionalist communists in the KPF, however, is that Stalinism was the only thing that guaranteed the survival of the tree for as long as it did. This issue will be dealt with more fully in the specific sections on the PDS.

3. Ibid., p. 6911. Also quoted in Gert Weisskirchen, 'Innere und äußere Zivilisierung. Die Opposition in der DDR und in Osteuropa' in Bernd Faulenbach et al. (eds), *Die Partei hatte immer recht. Aufarbeitung von Geschichte und Folgen der SED-Diktatur in Deutschland*, Essen, 1994, p. 189.
4. Usually translated as 'coming to terms with the past'.
5. Klaus von Dohnanyi, 'Gemeinsinn und Zivilcourage. Die Vergangenheit in der Zukunft Deutschlands', *Merkur*, no. 11, 2000, p. 1070.

The first question posed here, therefore, is whether it is indeed possible to identify a qualitative difference between Marxist promise and Stalinist reality.

The first problem we are confronted with is the fact that most of those writing on this question would maintain that there is no such difference and that Marxism and Stalinism are essentially one and the same. This elision takes place on two levels. First of all, on the generic level, Marxism and Stalinism are seen as identical. Secondly, on the specific level, Stalinism is seen as a monolithic phenomenon applicable to the whole of Eastern Europe in a very undifferentiated way. These two tendencies rest on two further factors.

The first is a historiographical and theoretical one: There is a trend, which can be traced back even to Marx's day, which understands his theory of history as being linear and teleological. The Hegelian influence on Marx is elevated until it becomes the only analytical basis for considering his theories of history. This means that the teleological elements in Marx are given absolute precedence over the voluntarist elements. According to this Stalino-Hegelian approach, history is an unstoppable iron wheel grinding on towards a pre-given communist future, somehow laid down in some putatively Marxist blueprint. From his very first political writings, however, Marx rejected this utopian and teleological approach. It is, after all, what led Marx himself to say to some French 'Marxists' at the end of the 1870s 'tout ce que je sais, c'est que moi, je ne suis pas marxiste'.[6]

Today this is still a dominant view of Marxism. Karen Leeder, for example, states that 'Marxism, as a materialist refinement of the Enlightenment belief in progress, *understood* [my emphasis, PT] history as a rationally transparent, dynamic and linear process, which would ultimately lead to the Communist goal.'[7] The use of the past tense 'understood' here is indicative in that it seems to imply that 'Marxism' is also something in the past tense and that it died with the GDR. Although the book is an excellent and nuanced exposition of the politics of the cultural opposition in the final years of the GDR, this sentence would seem to imply that the identification of Marxism with Stalinism has gone deep. Leeder points us to Joachim Streisand's book *Deutsche Geschichte von den Anfängen bis zur Gegenwart. Eine marxistische Analyse* as an example of a 'Marxist' interpretation of historical development and yet it is a standard Stalinist historiography, seeking to reify Marxism into an unalterable blueprint for all historical circumstances.[8] Streisand's interpretational

---

6. Friedrich Engels, 'Antwort an die Redaktion der Sächsischen Arbeiter-Zeitung', in Marx-Engels, *Werke*, vol. 22, Berlin, DDR, 1972, pp. 68–70.
7. Karen Leeder, *Breaking Boundaries. A New Generation of Poets in the GDR*, Oxford, 1996, p. 108.
8. Joachim Streisand, *Deutsche Geschichte von den Anfängen bis zur Gegenwart. Eine marxistische Analyse*, Cologne, 1976.

framework is classically monumentalist. His purpose, no matter how unconsciously, is to use Marx to kill Marx, to depoliticise and de-ideologise Marxism and reduce it to a sterile dogma designed merely to protect the GDR. In his hands Marx's materialist dialectic becomes a *Glücksrad der Geschichte* (history's wheel of fortune) – as the GDR poet Hans Brinkmann calls it – which indeed 'signal(s) the powerlessness of a lyric subject submitted to historical processes which appear meaningless'.[9]

Marx himself would have found historical processes as understood under Stalinism as meaningless as does Brinkmann. If Marx really did view communism as the end-point of an inevitable and linear historical process then why did he bother writing anything at all? What is the point of communist politics and of a manifesto for action if economic trends are anyway going to take the world there automatically? Why would he have written in his famous final thesis on Feuerbach, 'Philosophers have only interpreted the world in different ways. The point is, however, to change it' if all that was required was interpretation and patience?[10]

Marxism as Marx intended, however, sees history as being determined by both objective *and* subjective factors. The end result, therefore, is the product of the interaction between the objective and the subjective, each of which interpenetrates and changes the other. That is the whole point of the dialectic. Again, as he states in the *Eighteenth Brumaire*, 'People make their own history but not just as they please.'[11] Stalinist historiography is fundamentally non-dialectical as the change it envisages is firmly laid down in advance according to the general plan of the General Secretary and is anyway only valid for those societies which have yet to reach the state of Nirvana present in the Stalinist countries. For the Soviet Union under Stalin and the post-1945 'peoples' democracies' the end of the dialectic had already been reached and political change could not be tolerated. The irony of history, however, is that the collapse of communism in 1990 is one of the clearest examples of how the dialectic of history – as understood by Marx – functions in action, namely an interactive tension between economic base and political superstructure in which the latter worked as a brake on the development of the former and therefore had to be changed or swept away.

The second factor is an obvious one and is based in power politics. It is simply convenient for anti-socialist forces to contend that all forms of Marxism and socialism are dictatorial and authoritarian. The fundamental irony here, therefore, is that two diametrically opposed sets of enemies, namely pro-Western forces on the one side and pro-communist forces on the other, agree on what Marxism is. Just as with the anti-communist Right, the old guard of the Communist Parties always maintained that

---

9. Leeder, *Breaking Boundaries*, p. 110.
10. Marx-Engels, *Werke*, vol. 3, Berlin, DDR, 1969, p. 553.
11. Marx-Engels, *Werke*, vol. 8, Berlin, DDR, 1972, p. 116.

'Marxism-Leninism' was the logical conclusion of socialist development and represented the only possible path towards a communist society.

For Stalinists, the only impetus behind their thinking was the defence of the Soviet Union. Even those who were to become relatively critical of Soviet policy maintained an allegiance to the directives emanating from the Soviet leadership. If we read, for example, Wolfgang Leonhard's auto-biographical study of life in the KPD and later SED under Stalin, we gain a very clear picture of absolute loyalty to Moscow despite any reservations the individual may have about specific aspects of policy.[12] The shock wave which hit the international communist movement after Khrushchev's secret speech at the Twentieth Party Congress in 1956 was of such great magnitude precisely because of the blind loyalty to Stalin's Soviet Union that had preceded it.

On the other hand, and hardly surprisingly, anti-socialist forces in the West were always ready to agree with the Stalinists. For them it was and still is both a conviction and a political necessity to identify all forms of Marxism and socialism with the Soviet experience. This is then extended into an unsophisticated attempt to use totalitarian theory to equate the SED regime with that of the Nazi dictatorship so that all forms of social-ism can be equated with all forms of National Socialism. The next stage of the delegitimisation of social alternatives to capitalist state formations is to maintain that any attempt to uphold a utopian perspective or take a grand-narrative view of history will lead ineluctably to tyranny.[13] Liberal and conservative pragmatism therefore become the only valid and permissible contemporary political viewpoints.[14]

What is often left out of the equation with all of these studies, however, is the degree to which the 'SED dictatorship' was actually one forced upon the ex-GDR by the exigencies of the Cold War. In his book *Der vormund-schaftliche Staat* (The Authoritarian State) Rolf Henrich attempts to analyse the psychology of party and people in the GDR in terms of a need for authority. He points out that the SED also had a great need for clear polit-ical as well as psychological lines of authority from above and outside in the form of the Soviet Union.[15] As Sigried Meuschel maintains, the regime in the GDR was established purely under the auspices of Soviet Stalin-ism and not with any real self-determination.[16]

For the Left, the fundamental problem with Stalinism in Eastern Europe was that it was a regime which based itself upon a socio-economic set-up

12. Wolfgang Leonhard, *Die Revolution entläßt ihre Kinder*, Munich, 1980, p. 432.
13. See for example Christoph Dieckmann, 'Stalins Schädelstätte der 20 Millionen in seinen Lagern Ermordeten ist das Golgotha der Utopie', *Die Zeit*, no. 43, 19 October 2000, p. 11.
14. See, *Getrennte Vergangenheit, gemeinsame Zukunft*, vol. 4. See also Slavoj Žižek, *Did Somebody Say Totalitarianism? Four Interventions in the (Mis)use of a Notion*, London, 2001.
15. See Rolf Henrich, *Der vormundschaftliche Staat. Vom Versagen des real existierenden Sozialismus*, Reinbeck bei Hamburg, 1989.
16. Siegried Meuschel in *Getrennte Vergangenheit, gemeinsame Zukunft*, vol. 4, p. 36.

which was (at least in objective terms) post-capitalist and therefore also (at least in theory) progressive. And yet the political structures of the state, precisely because of the instability of control and resulting arbitrariness and authoritarianism, actually lagged behind the level of subjective political freedom afforded to workers in the capitalist states. Added to this dilemma was the fact that the longer the political system of Stalinism survived the more damage it did to the effectiveness of the planned economy. Taken together, these two factors mean that the neo-pragmatists who now rule in both East and West can maintain that despite whatever Marxism promises, the baby it delivers is always and ineluctably authoritarian and therefore 'Stalinist' as well as being inherently economically inferior to capitalism. Martin Amis's recent book about his father's and friends' flirtations with the Soviet Union follows the same unnuanced logic.[17]

On the other hand, those who adhere to some sort of anti-capitalist social and political programme will, of course, maintain that this is not the case and that it could have been different if, for example, the German revolution of 1918–19 had succeeded. Conservative forces, on the contrary, will argue that Stalinism was inherent in socialism from the very beginning.[18] The Left will then argue that the Soviet Union degenerated into Stalinism due to its isolation and that it then went on to impose deformed forms of socialism on other countries or zones of occupation, whose only role was to defend both militarily and politically the degeneration of the original model.[19] Given that this was the only form of socialism that has so far existed, neither side can claim any decisive insight on this matter. The Right can simply maintain that it will always be thus and the Left will maintain that it need not be. The Right has the advantage of contingency, the Left the apparent disadvantage of defeat.

For the Left, however, the responsibility for Stalinism lies at base quite clearly with capitalism. The dynamic of this analysis is an inverted form of the *Historikerstreit* (historians' dispute) of the early 1980s in Germany in which the Left tries to relativise Stalinism by pointing to the fact that the Soviet Union became what it was because of the threat of a rampant and successful Western imperialism. If Hitler was an understandable reaction to Bolshevism (a position which I do not hold) then certainly the perversion of Bolshevism into Stalinism can be seen as a reaction to the very real threat of Western intervention. In the context of this interpretation, the GDR can never be called an illegitimate state (*Unrechtsstaat*)

17. Martin Amis, *Koba the Dread: Laughter and the Twenty Million*, London, 2002.
18. In the words of Solzhenitzyn, 'the birth of the Gulag was announced by the shots of the battleship Aurora'. See also the contribution by Konrad Löw to the debate about the dictatorship of the proletariat in *Getrennte Vergangenheit, gemeinsame Zukunft*, vol. 1, pp. 100–110.
19. Leon Trotsky, *The Revolution Betrayed: What Is the Soviet Union and Where Is It Going?*, London, 1990.

because its very existence was contingent upon forces far beyond any autonomous, let alone universal, values of legitimacy (*Recht*) and illegitimacy (*Unrecht*). Rather, the GDR was determined by categories of Soviet power (*Macht*) and powerlessness (*Ohnmacht*).

If we read the many new studies arising from increased access to the Soviet and East German archives, then we can see – as with so much of this archival material – that it confirms much of what was already clear through the process of political deduction, namely, that the SBZ/GDR was entirely at the mercy of decisions taken in Moscow and within the SMAD. Of course, there was a degree of political autonomy for German Communists but it was limited. In that sense they made their own state but not in conditions of their own making. Norman Naimark, for example, points out that, as soon as the country was freed of fascism, the SMAD set about preventing any 'precipitate' attempts to set up a socialist Germany.[20] And yet in Wolfgang Leonhard's book, written well before the archives opened, we can see how the Ulbricht, Sobottka and Ackermann groups' first actions were to dissolve the spontaneous *Antifas* and to make sure there was no attempt at achieving socialism from below.[21] In those famous words, attributed to Walter Ulbricht, 'it has to look democratic but control must rest firmly in our hands'.

This, after all, is what 'real-existing socialism' meant. It was the admission that there was no alternative to the wrong road. The question posed within the PDS today, however, is whether there can be a form of socialism which can call itself radically anti-capitalist or Marxist but which can be seen to be relatively untainted by Stalinism. The further question which arises from this is whether the PDS can claim to be the vehicle for such a project. Or is it merely an organisation which, in terms of its attitude to the past, is undertaking 'an attempt a posteriori to give [it]self a history which [it] would like to have had, in contrast to that which [it] actually has'?[22]

Before looking at the PDS itself, however, it is necessary to look closely at the history of Stalinism in the GDR. What follows is an exposition of the social nature of the Soviet Union and the other Eastern European states and the relationship of the GDR with those states. These states were neither capitalist nor socialist but transitional. They represented degenerated (in the case of the Soviet Union) or deformed (in the case of the GDR and the rest of Eastern Europe) workers' states. The theoretical basis for this position rests on the fact that capitalism – understood as a system of generalised commodity production – was abolished in Eastern Europe as a result of the nationalisation of decisive parts of the means

20. Norman M. Naimark, *The Russians in Germany. A History of the Soviet Zone of Occupation, 1945–1949*, Cambridge, Mass., London, 1997.
21. Leonhard, *Die Revolution entläßt ihre Kinder*.
22. Nietzsche, *Werke und Briefe*, p. 3896.

of production, distribution and exchange. All processes of social repro-
duction were subordinated to the central plan and the plan was secured
against influences from the capitalist world by the creation of a monop-
oly of foreign trade. All of this took place, however, without creating
socialism as it was originally understood, namely as a democratically
planned economy based on the free association of the producers.

Political power in these states lay instead in the hands of a bureaucratic layer in the apparatuses of the party and the state. This layer did
not, however, represent an independent social class based on ownership
of the means of production. Rather, it was defined by its consumer privileges and its considerable decision-making capacity. This bureaucracy
was just as much in conflict with the working people of its own state as
it was with the West. It had to defend its social privileges and political
power against the former and the economic basis of its rule against the
latter. This means that there were indeed elements of socialism in the
facticity of post-capitalist forms of ownership, and yet social ownership
alone did not add up to socialism. As Wolf Biermann (the dissident East
German songwriter) put it at the Cologne concert in 1976, 'The people
own the factories, but who owns the people?'

The fact that the socio-economic basis of these societies was post-
capitalist meant political control was based upon social ownership and
was therefore nominally socialist. Its ruling layer in turn based the legit-
imisation of its power in socialist theory. To do otherwise was to admit
that socialism had failed and that there would have to be a return to the
law of value and recapitalisation, in which they would lose power unless
they could arrogate ownership of the means of production for themselves,
a tactic which they did follow after 1990 but at considerable personal
risk. The social instability of this layer is demonstrated by the fact that
its grip on power was indeed loosened so quickly when the end of
communism came about and that it was necessary for them to transform
themselves into property owners or nationalist tyrants in order to maintain influence in the post-socialist political realm.

However, there is one further complication in understanding Stalinism
in the GDR as distinct from the rest of Eastern Europe: namely, the
national question. For all of the other states of Eastern Europe, from the
Soviet Union via the non-Russian republics and the other Warsaw Pact
states, nationalism as a means of political control and popular mobilisation was an option which the ruling parties were always – and continue
to be – ready and able to use. The GDR, on the other hand, suffered from
its artificiality. It could never play the national communist card in the
same way as the other national communist parties could because it was
never a nation. It was not formed as the result of a revolution, national
uprising or plebiscite but was the product of power politics. The attempts
to create a GDR identity under Honecker were really only a rearguard

action in which social security and community in a decidedly Prussian tradition were emphasised, rather than some grandiose all-German nationalist project. The SED was always aware that to play the German card would immediately raise the issue of German unification. Alfred Kosing's pronouncements on the German road to socialism notwithstanding, the SED's political power was based on its subservience and absolute loyalty to the Soviet Union.[23] East German positions on the German national question were therefore decided in Moscow and not in Berlin, although again the decisions taken in Moscow were themselves conditioned by the state of play between the two main antagonists of the Cold War.

This form of bureaucratic internationalism allowed no space for national communist deviations in the GDR. Indeed, one of the reasons for the Soviet leadership's displeasure with Walter Ulbricht after 1968 was the worry that he was starting to attempt to play a GDR nationalist card along the lines of the Czech, Rumanian and Polish models. His proclamations of the model character of the GDR for the Eastern bloc and his ideas of socialism as an autonomous social formation only helped to reinforce this view. Above all, however, the popular base for national communism was fundamentally missing in the GDR. Attempts at creating a GDR identity failed almost completely. It is perhaps true to say that identification with the GDR is higher now than it was during its lifetime. Again, this paradox will be discussed below.

For this reason, the creation of a mythological history was even more important in the GDR than it was in those other countries where national heroes and myths could be mobilised for political purposes. There were two stages to this mythological approach to history. The first was the establishment of a pantheon of socialist martyrs. From Luxemburg to Thälmann, an anti-reactionary, anti-fascist mythology could be created. The GDR itself could be presented as the anti-fascist state *per se*, with the implication that that part of Germany had actually played a role in resisting Hitler to a greater extent than in West Germany. Emphasis was also always laid on the presence of ex-Nazis in prominent positions in the FRG as opposed to the thoroughgoing denazification which had taken place in the SBZ/GDR. The second approach, when it was perceived that the anti-fascist cause was not functioning in the way intended, was an attempt at creating an identification with more Prussian traditions.

These two approaches are illuminated by the Nietzschean categories outlined here, the first attempt representing a monumentalist approach, the second an antiquarian one. For the GDR, abstract socialist symbolism as an ideological tool was of central importance due to the absence of concrete examples of national heroes and movements.

---

23. Alfred Kosing, *Nation in Geschichte und Gegenwart*, Berlin, 1976.

There has always been a protracted war over the definition of terms going on within political and academic studies in the area of definitions of socialism, communism, Stalinism, neo-Stalinism and post-Stalinism. For example, Wolfgang Ruge takes a similar periodisation to the one I do for his definition of Stalinism and yet comes up with a different nomenclature.[24] He names this first period *klassischer Stalinismus* (classical Stalinism) and gives its dates as lasting from 1928 to 1953, that is, from the banning of the last vestiges of factional activity within the CPSU in the form of the Left Opposition up to Stalin's death.

Although the definition 'classical Stalinism' is acceptable, this period is too limited in that the Stalinisation of the CPSU demonstrably began before 1928, with the adoption of the policy of 'socialism in one country' as early as 1924. Along with this went the gradual removal of various individuals and groups from positions of power and influence within the CPSU. By 1928 the process of Stalinisation was largely completed, certainly as far as the Soviet Union was concerned and to a large extent the KPD as well. After Stalin's death too, there was only a gradual move away from the worst excesses of his rule and it was not until Khrushchev's secret speech that Stalin was criticised in any significant way. This was a criticism of the person, however, rather than the state and the political structures of bureaucratic rule, which remained firmly in place. Michael Nelken describes the difference thus:

> 'Stalinism' was not, for us, primarily about the cult of personality, show trials, terror and mass murder in the Soviet Union under Stalin. Rather it was about the crumbling political system in the GDR, about bureaucratism, centralism, administratism, arbitrary power. It was about the absence of democracy and the rule of law, an inefficient command economy, a prescribed intellectual and cultural life, the absence of a free press, freedom of speech and the freedom to travel.[25]

The desire to name the phenomenon after one particular person and to present its definition and its dates as concomitant with the political life span of that person is to misunderstand the fact that Stalinism was above all a social, rather than an individualised phenomenon. This is the major flaw in describing Khrushchev's secret speech at the Twentieth Congress of the CPSU as being about 'de-Stalinisation'. His attack on the cult of personality removed the monumentalist element of Stalinism but did not attack or change in any way its social base.

Stalinism can perhaps best be defined thus: It is the product of the isolation of a bureaucratic layer within the CPSU within a Soviet Union which was itself isolated by the failure of the world revolution which Lenin

24. Wolgang Ruge, 'Die Doppeldroge. Zu den Wurzeln des Stalinismus', in Rainer Eckert, Wolfgang Küttler and Gustav Seeber (eds), *Krise-Umbruch-Neubeginn. Eine kritische und selbstkritische Dokumentation der DDR Geschichtswissenschaft 1989/90*, Stuttgart, 1992, pp. 33–43, as quoted in Andreas Malycha, *Partei von Stalins Gnaden?*, Berlin, 1996.
25. Michael Nelken, 'Schwierigkeiten einer Emanzipation. Zur Stalinismusdebatte in der PDS', in Bisky et al., *Die PDS*, p. 67.

and Trotsky had hoped to bring about. This social layer gained material and political privileges which were based upon the social ownership of the productive forces. Its ideology therefore remained essentially social-ist in name as its power was based on that common ownership. As Christian Rakowsky points out:

> In a proletarian state, where capitalist accumulation is forbidden to the members of the ruling party, the differentiation is at first functional, but after-wards becomes social. I do not say it becomes a class differentiation, but a social one... The social situation of the communist who has at his disposition an automobile, a good apartment, regular vacations, and receives the party maximum of salary, differs from the situation of the communist who works in the coal mines, where he receives from 50 to 60 roubles a month.[26]

Thus Stalinism was not an ideology invented or introduced by Stalin, nor was it one which died with him, but was inherent in the backward-ness, defensiveness and isolation of an unfinished revolution. Its rule was by definition dictatorial as the transitional stage in which it became stuck due to its isolation was always bound to require authoritarian measures for its own defence. The measures introduced under Lenin and Trotsky as temporary survival strategies became, under Stalin, the ends rather than the means. Absolute subordination of the party and the workers to the rule of the General Secretary in the name of a discipline designed for a revolutionary period, in which there was no place for democratic exper-imentation, was carried over into a post-revolutionary period in which the consolidation of power replaced the struggle for power.

Stalin best represented this part of the bureaucracy within the leader-ship of the party and was able to consolidate his power on that basis. It is often maintained that Stalin merely continued the work which Marx and Lenin had started. If that were the case then the question has to be asked: why was it necessary for Stalin, within fourteen years of taking over the reins of power, to have physically eliminated all of the other revolutionary Bolshevik leaders as well as millions of ordinary party members? Using the theory of monumentalisation we can show that to do so in the name of Marx and Lenin does not prove the continuum but can actually be seen to disprove it.

This brings us to the second reason for applying Nietzschean categories: namely, that the actual ideological and psychological processes involved in incorporating but also destroying the original critical Marxist and Leninist impulses behind the revolutionary workers' movement have to be under-stood properly before the tenacity and longevity of a degenerated official and reified Marxism-Leninism can be analysed. The consequences of this longevity for the PDS are also, therefore, of central importance as the party

---

26. Christian Rakowsky in Leon Trotsky, *The Revolution Betrayed.*
   http://csf.colorado.edu/mirrors/marxists.org/archive/trotsky/works/1936-rev/ch05.ht
   m#ch05-1.

is faced with the task of rejecting the latter reified version and rediscovering the former critical version of their own history.

On this basis we can say that what Ruge defines as high or classical Stalinism (1928–53) represented monumentalism in both physical and metaphorical form. While he lived, Stalin promoted a cult of the personality around himself and elevated and reified Marx and Lenin into the quasi-religious figures around whom the dogma of Marxism-Leninism could be erected. He did so in order to create from the measures which grew out of the chaos of the revolution and the civil war a loyal and supine bureaucracy which could be bent to his will. His greatness, however, existed only in standing on the mausoleums of great men.

Monumentalism

The monumental uses great figures of the past in order to serve the present. It takes figures and creates myths out of them. It elevates them and reifies them into something which serves as a model for imitation. As Nietzsche puts it, 'If a person wishing to build great things needs the past at all then he will use monumentalist history to do so.'[27]

Despite what this quotation might seem to imply, however, the use of great monumental figures from the past was not a simple mechanism for creating a straightforward sense of inspiration in the popular imagination. The psychological processes Nietzsche saw as taking place were in fact far more subtle than that. For him, great figures from the past were taken as inspirational figures but only by emasculating what they actually stood for first. By monumentalising someone they are also reified, made safe, defused and controlled. As Günter Kunert says: 'in both Soviet and German socialism there were only over-dimensional heroes'.[28]

Marxism-Leninism was introduced as the official theoretical basis of the Soviet state in 1938, a year after the great purge in which many millions of loyal communists were killed or banished in the name of the fight against 'Trotskyism'. An insight into the psychological processes behind this can be found in the following quotation from Nietzsche where we see his definition of how monumental history can be used to kill off the original intentions of those being reified:

> Monumental history is the theatrical costume in which they pretend that their hate for the powerful and the great of their time is a fulfilling admiration for the strong and the great of past times. In this, through disguise they invert the real sense of that method of historical observation into its opposite. Whether they know it or not, they certainly act as if their motto were: let the dead bury the living.[29]

27. Nietzsche, *Werke und Briefe*, p. 3886.
28. Günter Kunert, 'Der verschlagene Biedermann', *Der Spiegel* no. 37, 13 September 1999
29. Nietzsche, *Werke und Briefe*, p. 3886. Translation by Ian C. Johnston.

At first sight this quotation would not seem to be entirely appropriate for a description of the mechanisms going on within Stalinism. The whole point of Stalinism, surely, is that the monumentalists are the 'powerful and the great' of their time. However, if we see the bureaucracy as a social layer which exists only as an administrative body whose hold on power and greatness is entirely political and arbitrary and not based on the traditional class security of the material ownership of property, then the very existence of their power and greatness is constantly under threat. The ideology which puts them into positions of power within the state is also an ideology which sees power and the state as transient and transitional entities which are to wither away automatically when their work is done. There are therefore two sources of insecurity for the socialist bureaucrat: the theoretical and the practical. Furthermore there are, within these two categories, two further sources of insecurity, namely, the short and the long term.

On the theoretical level, the communist movement is based organisationally on the concept of democratic centralism. This essentially means that all party functionaries are to be elected and controlled from below. They are under constant observation; they have a duty to present themselves for regular approval of their work and can be removed by a vote at any time. In addition they are to be rotated in their functions so that they do not become a professional bureaucracy and are limited in their wages to the level of a skilled manual worker so that they do not gain material privilege from their position. This is the democratic element of control from below. The centralist element rests on the fact that, once a decision has been made as a result of the democratic process, then it is the duty of all members of the party to carry out and support that decision regardless of whether they agree with it. Strict party discipline was seen as vitally important in a revolutionary period in which the groundwork for the establishment of the dictatorship of the proletariat was being laid. These principles were first outlined by Marx as a result of the experience of the Paris Commune of 1871.

There is a further element to Marxist theories of the state which maintains that, once social contradictions and classes have been removed under a communist society in which there is an abundance of goods, then there will be no need for a state at all. (Trotsky described the traditional authoritarian state as the policeman at the head of a bread queue. If there is no queue, then there is no need for a policeman. If there is no bread, then more policemen are needed.)

For these reasons, in theory at least, the material attractions of actually being involved in the bureaucratic functions of running a transitional socialist state are severely limited. Only those who have an ideological commitment to the undermining and eventual removing of their own functions would be attracted to such a role as there is no chance of material enrichment in the short term. Nor, essentially, is there the possibility of passing on material privilege to any future progeny in the long term.

On the practical level, the isolation of the Russian revolution soon meant that the democratic element of democratic centralism itself withered away and only the centralist element of party discipline was left. This element now became the organising principle of the bureaucratic layer which grew out of and took control of the party. Any democratic control from below was replaced by loyalty to the upper echelons of the party. On this level too, the two temporal insecurities were also present in the Soviet bureaucracy: Firstly, in the short term, one's job (indeed, one's life) was at the arbitrary disposal of the level above rather than the level below. This resulted in a loyalty to authority rather than to the revolution. Secondly, in the long term, the party became the state and the defence of the state required loyalty to the party.

The authoritarian tendencies which are necessarily inherent in any revolutionary movement were therefore brought out much more forcefully by the stalling of the revolution. The authoritarian tendency within the Bolshevik Party, which was necessary to make a revolution, could also come to destroy the revolution. Trotsky's most important insight here was to compare the French and Russian revolutions and to describe Stalin's rule as a new form of the Bonapartist Thermidor: that is, that it was based on the revolution and yet had to cripple the progressive dynamic of the revolution in order to survive. In this sense, we can say that Stalinism was counter-revolutionary in the name of the revolution, a form of Counter-Reformation.

The discipline that this sleight of hand required was equally valid for all layers of the party right up to the level of the General Secretary who, in Stalin, represented absolute power in the state. Loyalty to Stalin was loyalty to the party which in turn was also loyalty to the state and to the revolution. In order to obtain this loyalty it was necessary to consolidate state power in the name of the revolutionary overthrow of state power. It was therefore also necessary to build a theoretical basis for consolidation in the works of those in whose name the revolution had taken place. The theory of socialism in one country and the presence of a powerful imperialist enemy provided perfect justification for the consolidation and reification of power as an end in itself.

As a result of this development, the role of the communist parties outside the Soviet Union soon became one of absolute defence of the Bolshevik Party/CPSU and, of course, of the Soviet Union itself. After 1924 we can see quite clearly that the Soviet attitude to revolutionary movements in the rest of the world was extremely cautious, if not directly counter-revolutionary. The bureaucracy could not tolerate an alternative pole of attraction for the international working class and was always far more hostile to other working-class parties than to bourgeois or even fascist ones. This transition from revolutionary internationalism to bureaucratic consolidation can be found in the theoretical works of Stalin himself around 1924. Michael Löwy points out that, as late as May 1924, Stalin was still adhering to the theory of international revolution and Russia's role in it by writing: 'For the final victory of socialism, for the organisation of socialist production, the efforts of one country, particularly a peasant country like Russia, are insufficient; for that the efforts of the proletariat of several advanced countries are required.'[30] Only a few months later, after strengthening his own position in the leadership, he wrote that the USSR was ready to 'push on with the organising of a socialist economy'.[31]

The list of revolutions opposed or betrayed by the Stalinist bureaucracy is long and well documented elsewhere.[32] From China in 1925–28, Spain in 1936, Yugoslavia, China and Vietnam in 1945–48, Cuba in 1958 and Indonesia in 1966 through to the uprisings in Western Europe in 1968, the role of the communist parties in those countries was to undermine, stall and divert revolutionary potential. This was always done ostensibly because of the Soviet view that conditions were not yet ripe for revolution. The real Soviet motivation, however, was to prevent a loss of bureaucratic control over the international communist movement.

To understand the SED – and consequently the PDS – as parties it is necessary to recognise that the Stalinisation of the GDR actually began in 1924, a quarter of a century before its foundation. The process of monumentalism therefore spread from the top of the Soviet party down through the ranks. It began as the means of cementing the ideological justification for dictatorial rule and then spread outwards into the rest of the world communist movement as a means of controlling all developments in the name of the defence of the October Revolution.

Antiquarianism

Although the cult of personality around Stalin was gradually removed after his death in 1953, the actual functional mechanisms for his rule remained firmly in place. There was a limited liberalisation of some aspects of the Soviet bloc states but it stayed well within the parameters of the interests of bureaucratic rule. It would perhaps be better to speak of this second period as neo-Stalinism. I use the term antiquarianism to define it here.

30. Josef Stalin, *On the Opposition (1921–1927)*, as quoted in Michael Löwy, *The Politics of Combined and Uneven Development. The Theory of Permanent Revolution*, London, 1981, p. 70.
31. Ibid., p. 71.
32. Ibid.

Again, as Meuschel points out, most of the work done to consolidate the GDR was undertaken after Stalin's death and after the process of so-called de-Stalinisation had already begun.[33] She therefore also maintains that it is very difficult to fix the GDR within a traditional totalitarian framework. By this I take her to mean that the GDR was, from its very beginning, essentially a neo-Stalinist or antiquarian state formation, rather than a high-Stalinist or monumentalist one. Given the international system of power after 1945 and the way in which the two halves of Germany were situated on the front line of this inter-systemic conflict, it would have been very difficult for Stalin to have imposed his rule in all its Soviet brutality. In any case, the high point of monumentalist Stalinism was passed in the Soviet Union and the need to rebuild the country took precedence. This meant that concessions had to be made in the Soviet Zone of Occupation which required at least a formal adherence to questions of democratic development and national unity. The social base and security of the emerging East German bureaucracy in the form of the KPD leadership were actually strengthened by the end of terroristic monumentalism and the shift to conservative antiquarianism. The antiquarian approach is one in which he who 'understands only how to conserve life and not to create it'[34] is in charge. It is conservative, obsessed with control and detail and with rejecting anything which could destabilise existing conditions. Antiquarian history is used by one who 'wishes to live only in the familiar and the accustomed'.[35]

The consolidation of the Soviet Union and the Eastern Bloc after Stalin's death represents an essentially antiquarian use of history and social control. This trend was even further deepened after 1964 in the Brezhnev and Honecker era. Their social conservatism was matched only by their petty bureaucratism. The Brezhnev/Honecker era is now widely seen as one of relative stability as well as stagnation and it is largely to this period that any true nostalgic appeals to the past are made. Ironically there is perhaps no more accurate description of Honecker's attitude to the GDR and the apparent nostalgia for the Honecker years than the one to be found in the following quotation from Nietzsche:

> History belongs secondly to the man who preserves and honours, to the person who with faith and love looks back in the direction from which he has come, where he has been. Through this reverence he, as it were, gives thanks for his existence. While he nurtures with a gentle hand what has stood from time immemorial, he wants to preserve the conditions under which he came into existence for those who are to come after him. And so he serves life. His possession of his ancestors' goods changes the ideas in such a soul, for those goods are far more likely to take possession of his soul. The small, limited, crumbling, and archaic keep their own worth and integrity, because the

---

33. Meuschel in *Getrennte Vergangenheit, Gemeinsame Zukunft*, vol. 1., p. 36.
34. Nietzsche, *Werke und Briefe*, p. 3893.
35. Ibid., p. 3887.

conserving and honouring soul of the antiquarian man settles on these things and there prepares for itself a secret nest. The history of his city becomes for him the history of his own self. He understands the walls, the turreted gate, the dictate of the city council, and the folk festival, like an illustrated diary of his youth, and he rediscovers for himself in all this his force, his purpose, his passion, his opinion, his foolishness, and his bad habits. He says to himself, here one could live, for here one may live, and here one can go on living, because we endure and do not collapse overnight. Thus, with this "We" he looks back over the past amazing lives of individuals and feels himself like the spirit of the house, the generation, and the city. From time to time he person-ally greets from the far away, obscure, and confused centuries the soul of a people as his own soul, with a feeling of completion and premonition, a scent of almost lost tracks, an instinctively correct reading even of a past which has been written over, a swift understanding of the erased and reused parchments (which have, in fact, been erased and written over many times).[36]

In this context the antiquarian nature of GDR ideology, under Honecker especially, once again becomes apparent. Reading Nietzsche's words, one is strongly reminded of the sorts of speeches Honecker regularly made at the annual anti-fascist commemorations of Luxemburg, Liebknecht and Thälmann. The SED's main task after the uncertainties about the German question following Stalin's death and the subsequent workers' uprising was to conserve and consolidate Soviet power.[37] The SED was the ideal agency for this task because the KPD had already, almost from its very beginning, been a thoroughly Stalinised organisation.[38] As the KPD grad-ually came to dominate the SED after the turn to the *Partei des neuen Typs* (new type party – i.e. Marxist-Leninist) in 1947/48, so the Stalinisation of the SBZ/GDR could be deepened. This process was compounded by the fact that the socio-economic changes which took place in the SBZ/GDR were not primarily the result of internal but of external factors. The attempt by Ackermann to make a virtue out of the fact that the objec-tive conditions for the establishment of socialism in Germany had been brought about by the Red Army was never convincing. Moreover, it went entirely against the Marxist dictum that 'the liberation of the working class must always be carried out by the working class itself'. Vulgar econ-omistic objectivism was therefore present in the Stalinist self-understanding of the GDR from the very first days, even amongst those traditionally seen as less Stalinist than others.

Dieter Segert, for example, divides the GDR into a revolutionary and a post-revolutionary use of terror, with the building of the wall as the turning-point.[39] This seems to be correct as far as the chronology of the

---

36. Ibid., p. 3888.
37. Rudolf Herrnstadt, *Das Herrnstadt-Dokument. Das Politbüro der SED und die Geschichte des 17. Juni 1953*, Reinbeck bei Hamburg, 1990.
38. See Hermann Weber, *Aufbau und Fall einer Diktatur*, Cologne, 1991; Malycha, *Partei von Stalins Gnaden?*
39. Dieter Segert, 'Was war die DDR? Schnitte durch ihr politisches System', *Berliner Debatte INITIAL*, no. 2/3, vol. 9, 1998, p.8.

use of physical and ideological terror is concerned but it misdiagnoses the concept of revolutionary and post-revolutionary developments. The point is that there was no revolution in East Germany and the uses of terror and coercion were contingent upon relations between the super-powers and the USSR's need for stability above revolutionary conflict. As such, his account does not really address the issues of why this change came about and what its background was.

The Stalinisation which took place in the GDR after 1949 could not be the same raw version which had prevailed in the Soviet Union for the previous 25 years. There were two reasons for this. Firstly the material position of the Soviet Union had been seriously weakened by the fight against Hitler. Some 20 million Soviet dead and the laying waste of major cities and agricultural production in the west of the Soviet Union meant that Stalin had to keep open the possibility of continued cooperation with the West in order to earn a breathing space for reconstruction and repa-rations from the Western zones of occupation. This meant that the immediate and primary Soviet priority was not for the establishment of a Soviet-style system but for one with some vestiges of political open-ness.[40]

Secondly, the SPD soon emerged at the end of the war as the most popular representative of the working class. For obvious political reasons it was not possible for Stalin to immediately attack the SPD and to drive it underground. Instead, a process of cooperation was established, which soon switched, however, to one of co-option and then coercion. The measures taken were typical of classical monumentalist Stalinism, involv-ing arbitrary arrests, imprisonment and even some executions. However, the open border, the continuing strength of social democratic workers, Stalin's death and the workers' uprising of 1953 all gave rise to the need for concessions towards the working class. Once the policy of the radical dismantling of GDR industry and the payment of reparations from current production in the form of Soviet Joint-Stock Companies came to an end in 1953, the shift from classical to neo-Stalinism, from monumentalism to antiquarianism, was well under way. Stalin's successors in Moscow, after the short lived Beria regime, which tested the possibility of the aban-donment of the GDR as a tactical step, soon realised that if the decision were to be taken to consolidate power in Eastern Europe and the GDR in particular, it would have to be done on a very different basis. I shall discuss in the next chapter how this ideological shift fitted in with

---

40. There is exhaustive material available on this, for example: Peter Brandt and Herbert Ammon, *Die Linke und die nationale Frage*, Reinbeck bei Hamburg, 1981; Peter Brandt and Herbert Ammon, *Die Deutsche Einheit kommt bestimmt*, Bergisch Gladbach, 1982; Joseph Foschepoth (ed.), *Kalter Krieg und Deutsche Frage*, Göttingen and Zurich, 1985; Joseph Foschepoth, (ed.) *Adenauer und die Deutsche Frage*, Göttingen and Zürich, 1988, amongst many others.

changes in the situation of the global economy and the consequent relations between East and West.

The interesting thing about the infamous 1953 CDU poster which
stated that 'All Marxist roads lead to Moscow', therefore, was that
Moscow wholeheartedly agreed with it. Those in the West who used that
slogan, however, are today happy to attribute sole blame for the authoritarian nature of the GDR to the SED and, by extension, to the PDS.
Conversely, when members of the PDS defend the role of the SED in the
GDR, they often unconsciously use the same 1953 slogan as supporting
and mitigating evidence. Herbert Mayer states, for example: 'Of course
the Stalinisation of the SED cannot be seen as the outcome of the Cold
War.'[41] Certainly, if one considers the Cold War to date simply from the
date of the introduction of the Truman doctrine between March and June
1947, as does Mayer, then this could perhaps be argued. However, if one
sees the introduction of the Truman doctrine as simply the newest round
in an ongoing inter-systemic battle between East and West going back to
1917, as I shall argue in the next chapter, then the Long Cold War is
indeed the basis for the Stalinisation of the SED in that its controlling
element, the KPD, was already thoroughly Stalinised by the mid 1920s.
In the case of Stalinism too, it should be remembered, 1945 was not some
sort of Zero Hour, but represented continuity rather than a break.

However, in the documents and evidence given to the Enquête-
Kommission which was set up after 1989 to enquire into guilt and
responsibility in the GDR, the constant impression one gains is of the
way in which those who carried out any functions in the GDR did so
within constraints laid down not only from above but from outside the
GDR in the form of the Soviet Union.[42] As the Tulpanow memorandum
demonstrates, the SED was turned into a Stalinist organisation in the late
1940s because it found itself 'at the border between two worlds, where
the capitalist world meets the socialist world. That is why it is burdened
with such great tasks.'[43] There was, of course, also some resistance to
this policy from within the leadership of the Soviet Union and those
around Semjonow attempted to maintain a more open position on the
question of German unification. The only real conclusion we can draw,
however, is that the Soviet approach was multifaceted and at all times
designed to protect the interests of the Soviet Union and therefore
changed with changes in the global political situation.

The operative and destructive word in the Tulpanow memorandum,
however, is 'burdened'. This shows that the initial openness was replaced

---

41. Herbert Mayer, *Nur eine Partei nach Stalins Muster? Weichenstellungen für die SED im Jahre
    1948*, Berlin, 1998. p. 14.
42. See, for example, Egon Bahr's fascinating testimony to the Enquête-Kommision, *Getren-
    nte Vergangenheit, gemeinsame Zukunft*, vol. 3, pp. 147–154.
43. Quoted from Malycha, *Partei von Stalins Gnaden?*, p. 93.

by a harder, more pro-division line after the shift to the Truman Doctrine in the U.S. in 1947 and the Yugoslav crisis of 1948, and that Soviet policy towards Germany was largely determined by reactions to external factors in the developing Cold War and did not exist in any predetermined and identifiable long-term plan. This is shown in 1953 when the death of Stalin led to the assumption of leadership for a short period by Beria who was essentially determined to abandon the GDR in favour of improved relations with the West. The uprising that this policy change in part provoked sealed the fate of the Left's hopes for German unification in that the Soviet Union could not possibly afford to lose the GDR for fear of a reverse domino effect – precisely what did happen in 1989/90.

Naturally there was a degree of relative autonomy for GDR functionaries but the reality of that autonomy was that it was often used in order to please rather than challenge the Soviet masters. At the risk of moving into the realms of moral equivalence, the concept developed by Ian Kershaw of 'working towards the Führer' can also be applied to the SED, which continuously 'worked towards' the CPSU. Under both Ulbricht and Honecker, it was absolutely necessary for the GDR to play the role of the model pupil. The extent to which the Soviet Union determined the policy of the SED can be seen in the example of Ulbricht's resignation and his replacement with Honecker.

On 21 January 1971, thirteen of the twenty members of the Politbüro wrote a letter designated as a 'highly confidential matter' to Brezhnev, in which they demanded Ulbricht's removal as First Secretary of the Central Committee on the following grounds;

> Unfortunately we can no longer ignore the fact that Comrade Walter Ulbricht, in any case a difficult personality, has recently been showing increasingly negative character defects. His distance from the real life of the party, the working class and all working people is matched only by his descent into unrealistic dreaming and subjectivism. His attitude to his Politburo comrades and others is often rude and insulting and he only discusses matters from a position of apparent infallibility.[44]

They further asked him to force Ulbricht to step down 'voluntarily' for health reasons, which Brezhnev did on 12 April 1971. On 27 April Ulbricht announced his 'retirement' in a text which had, again, already been cleared with Brezhnev.

In contrast, it is only with the shift to Gorbachov's policy of the Common European Home in the late 1980s that the GDR becomes a stumbling-block rather than a model pupil. For example, Datchitchov (a former Soviet Ambassador to the GDR) points out that when Gorbachov made his secret speech at the summit of all the socialist countries in November 1986 – in which he called for the relations to be returned to a normal basis in which all states would be equal – Honecker resisted

---

44. Website *Die DDR im WWW*, http://www.ddr-im-www.de/index2.htm

this idea. As Datchitchov points out, 'It became clear that it was not in his [Honecker's] interest at all to surrender the guarantee of security which the Soviet Union had always provided in the form of the Brezhnev Doctrine.' It is clear that from that date onwards Honecker collaborated with hard-line anti-Gorbachov forces in the Soviet Union around Ligachov in order to halt the development of a common European home, which he was aware would inexorably lead to the end of the Berlin Wall.[45]

That this can be seen as both a positive as well as a negative thing can be seen from Ellen Brombacher's rather contradictory interpretation of GDR history. On the one hand she agrees that the SED made many mistakes but that this was due to the SED's dependence on the Soviet Union. However, she then describes Gorbachov's policies in the mid 1980s in which the ties between the Soviet Union and the GDR were loosened, as 'treason':

> That the SED was largely responsible [for the deep crisis in the GDR] is clear. But we cannot reduce all of the causes of this crisis to internal factors. At least two further components essential to the collapse of the GDR have to be taken into account. The GDR could not survive other than in alliance with the Soviet Union. This alliance was effectively terminated, not in so many words but by the normative power of Soviet actions. I suspect that Gorbachov's policies in those years were motivated not least by the illusion that he would be rewarded by the West for selling out his allies. In that context I think the word 'treachery' is appropriate.[46]

In this reading the GDR is seen as having no reason to exist other than as an outpost of the Soviet Union, but also that any change in that status brought about by the Soviet Union amounts to treachery. What greater proof does one need for the artificial nature and dependence of the GDR than this quotation from someone from the hard-line KPF faction within the PDS? Whether or not one agrees with her assertion that Gorbachov was a traitor, the central point is made, that the socialism the GDR represented was one which only existed because of the Soviet Union. Otto Reinhold, chief ideologist of the SED in the 1980s, said the same thing in August 1989 when he maintained that:

> The GDR can only exist as an anti-fascist, socialist state, as a socialist alternative to West Germany. What reason would a capitalist GDR have to exist next door to a capitalist West Germany? None, of course. Only if we remember this does it become clear that our strategy must be based on an uncompromising defence of the socialist order in the GDR.[47]

These quotations show us the extent to which the leaders of the GDR were aware of the artificiality and therefore vulnerability of their state. It

45. *Getrennte Vergangenheit, gemeinsame Zukunft*, vol. 3, p. 103.
46. Ellen Brombacher, 'Zum Sonderparteitag vom Dezember 1989', in Bisky et al., *Die PDS*, pp. 147–150 (here p. 148).
47. As quoted in Renata Fritsch-Bournazel, *Europa und die deutsche Einheit*, Bonn, 1990, pp. 114–115.

is no wonder that they saw Gorbachov as a traitor. And yet the question as to whether they themselves were betraying socialism by sticking to an artificial, real existing model is perhaps of more relevance. It is rather akin to accusing a doctor who switches off a life-support machine for someone in a vegetative coma of being a murderer. That, too, is often a religious objection.

How do we explain the ideological manoeuvres of a bureaucratic layer in consolidating their own positions of power on the basis of an incomplete or degenerated form of the original intentions of the socialist project? Trotsky had already addressed this issue in his work *The Revolution Betrayed*, where he stated that eventually the bureaucracy either would be overthrown by a revolutionary force or would transform itself into a property-owning class. The first would require a political revolution without removing the socialised nature of production, distribution and exchange. The second would require a social as well as a political revolution, in which the bureaucracy itself would control developments in its own interests. The first would require a complete purging of the bureaucracy by the new regime, the second merely a bureaucratic transfer of ownership. The second course is undoubtedly what came about in the Soviet Union after 1991.

However, for the bureaucracy in the GDR, the options of post-communist nationalism or capitalist property ownership were not available because the national dimension could be diverted and soaked up into the process of German unification and the transfer of property took place not on an indigenous basis but from outside, this time from the West rather than the East. In Russia and Eastern Europe major layers of the bureaucracy simply handed state property over to themselves. In the GDR the expropriators were expropriated by the expropriators in the form of the Treuhandanstalt (The state holding company appointed after 1990 to privatise state assets). Even here, many formerly loyal party members and enterprise directors were very easily able to maintain their positions of power and turn them into positions of wealth. This trend was partially undermined by the shock therapy imposed on the GDR by the terms of the unification treaty in which economic and monetary union and the activities of the Treuhandanstalt resulted in the collapse of the already weak East German industry.

So we can say that, paradoxically, it is the leaders of the West who seek to legitimise the GDR retrospectively in order that they may heap political opprobrium on the leaders of the SED and, by association, the PDS, whilst those who most fiercely supported the GDR such as Krenz, Brombacher and Reinhold, seek – perhaps understandably – to delegitimise or relativise it retrospectively by pointing out its subservience to Soviet diktat.

Critical History

The critical approach is just that. It takes history and subjects all of its aspects to a radical criticism. However, it does not do this just as some sort of academic exercise, but in order to change the present. As Nietzsche put it, 'only he who feels a tightness in his chest and an overwhelming need to unburden himself will also feel the need for critical history'.[48] During the period from 1924 onwards it should be pointed out that, in addition to the Stalinist *apparatchiks*, there were many critical elements within the workers' movement who had to use history in order to throw off the present and, in a very real sense, continue to live and hope for the future. These forces existed within the movement itself, from the Trotskyists to the social democrats to the reform communists around Nagý and Dubček via Havemann and Biermann to Gorbachov, and they all had a historical as well as a political approach to their criticisms of the system.

The GDR was not, therefore, simply a national variant of the 'bureaucratic-Stalinist society in transition from capitalism to socialism' but was, through its nationally fragmented nature and its unique position between the power blocs, a deformed society whose development was affected by special conditions not present in the rest of Eastern Europe. Any serious analysis of the GDR, its opposition and the state of the Left during and after reunification has to accept these political realities.

Rainer Land and Ralf Possekel address precisely this issue in their book *Fremde Welten*, which deals with the paradox of two groups of Left oppositionists within and outside the SED who had very similar views on questions of policy but who were unable to cooperate because of historical differences and differences over history.[49] As they point out:

> As early as 1990 we suspected that the reasons for the barriers to communication lay neither in considerations of programmatic demands nor in the character of the individuals involved. Rather they were to be found in the collectively accepted patterns of interpretation and action which are more fundamental than programmatics and which are mythologised by reference to straightforward political values.[50]

Land and Possekel further identify three critically discursive groups within the communist tradition and the SED.[51]

The first were the so-called *Altkommunisten* (old communists), whose historical codes were formed out of periods of exile, prison and concentration camps under the Nazis and who had a moral attachment to the

48. Ibid. This is, presumably, what Leonhard also refers to as 'Bauchschmerzen' in his novel *Die Revolution entläßt ihre Kinder* cited elsewhere here.
49. Rainer Land and Ralf Possekel, *Fremde Welten. Die gegensätzliche Deutung der DDR durch SED-Reformer und Bürgerbewegung in den 80er Jahren*, Berlin, 1998.
50. Ibid., pp. 8–9.
51. Ibid., pp. 10–11.

concept of a German socialism. Their discourse was determined by three historical debates in the GDR, which I have already outlined above. They were the Ackermann debate in 1945, the *New Course* debate in 1953 and the de-Stalinisation debate of 1956.

The second was the *Aufbaugeneration* (the reconstruction generation), whose discourse was largely determined by technocratic debates about the NÖSPL of 1963 and the Czech reform course of 1968. They were primarily concerned with reforms which would stabilise the existing system and allow it to realise what was thought to be its full potential at the time.

The third was the *Konspirativer Avantgarde* (conspiratorial avant-garde) within the SED, which began in the mid-1970s and which included groups such as the Democratic Communists and those who, noting the onset of deep economic crisis in the world – and predominantly Soviet – economic systems, were searching for new directions within socialism which would allow it to change and adapt.[52]

In fact the categories Land and Possekel differentiate here fit in precisely with my definition of monumentalist, antiquarian and critical approaches. What they also demonstrate, however, is that the categories are themselves in flux and cannot be strictly delineated. All three of them, although clearly existing within their self-defined parameters are also each of them in their own way critical. Their attitudes towards the state and society of the GDR were essentially loyal but tempered by a readiness to recognise the severe limitations that system imposed upon itself and had had imposed upon it. Indeed their main weapon of attack on the system was often not one of alternative economic policies or social programmes but of interpretations of history and of who was the true possessor of and successor to the communist tradition. Starting with the Khrushchev secret speech at the Twentieth Party Congress and ending with Gorbachov's attempts to wrest history from the grip of the monumentalists and the antiquarians in the late 1980s, a consideration of the past has been a central concern of the critical Left. The example of the banning of the Soviet historical magazine *Sputnik* by the GDR authorities in 1987 because of its reconsideration of the role of the KPD in the 1930s shows the extent to which the control of history is about the control of the present.

All of the Eastern European states varied in important socio-economic and historico-cultural respects which, naturally, have to be integrated into any analysis of Stalinism. In relation to the GDR, we could make the following points about how it differed significantly from its Eastern European neighbours such as its relatively high degree of industrialisation, its strong socialist and communist traditions and its predominantly Protestant

52. For a comprehensive list of archive material on the reform debate in the SED visit the following website: http://berlinerdebatte.sireco.de/projekte/sed/sed.htm

confessional composition. However, this is not sufficient for a proper analysis of the GDR as it was different from the other Eastern European states in ways which went far beyond the various qualities of 'normal' national differences and which separated it out from Poland, Hungary and the other states. The critical opposition in the GDR was essentially left-wing in its approach and was critical of Stalinist Marxism in the name of a true socialism for the following reasons:

1. The relationship to the Soviet Union. The GDR emerged from the SBZ after the military defeat of Germany in the Second World War and was dominated by this factor to the very end of its existence. For example, 400,000 Soviet troops were stationed in the GDR (incomparably more than in any other Eastern European state, where Soviet presence was, by the 1980s, either symbolic or even, as in the case of Romania, non-existent) who had the right in law to intervene in the affairs of the GDR up to and including the internationally recognised right of military intervention. The limited sovereignty of the GDR thus lay not just in the de facto nature of the Brezhnev doctrine as it applied to the rest of Eastern Europe but was anchored in international constitutional law. Questions of the status of Berlin, of reunification and of the four-power status of the administration of Germany were present right up until the Unification Treaty of 1990.

2. The central strategic importance of the GDR for the Soviet Union meant that it was inconceivable that it should have undertaken reforms without direct permission and encouragement from Moscow. It was therefore impossible, for example, for the SED leadership to implement bureaucratic nationalist campaigns with anti-Russian undertones à la Gomulka and Ceaucescu in order to strengthen its own internal legitimacy and to win greater breathing-space for its own domestic and foreign policy agendas. Equally important, however, is the fact that the recognition of the impossibility of fundamental change without the permission of the Soviet Union also dominated the thinking of the opposition groups in the GDR, both inside and outside the SED.

3. All of the other Eastern European states possessed a historically conditioned national or multinational identity which formed the 'natural framework' for their political development. Internal political crises perhaps threatened the stability of the regime but not the actual continued existence of the state as such. Whatever was to happen in the rest of Eastern Europe, the states there would never be under threat of disappearing completely from the map. The GDR's very existence, however, was always threatened by any oppositional activity because throughout its whole history it was never clear that the majority of the people would not vote for reunification with the neighbouring, bigger, richer, capitalist Federal Republic, if they had the

chance. Despite what was said throughout the years by the apologists for the division of Germany, the SED was always aware of this fundamental reality in all their political calculations.

These fundamental realities also underpin all of the superficial contentions often found about the absence of a 'Right' opposition in the GDR, the essentially 'leftist' orientation of its dissidents and its overwhelmingly proletarian social character. Despite all of these very real factors it could not be ignored that the threat of revolution may have existed only externally in the form of the Federal Republic but that actually the threat was much more real than in the other East European states. The omnipresent influence of the FRG in the form of radio, television and family connections made the GDR, on the one hand, the most 'open', best-informed and most Western-oriented society in the Soviet bloc. On the other hand, however, this strong external pressure and the constant latent presence of the question of reunification prevented the 'normal' and 'organic' development of internal political contradictions because of the 'fortress mentality' to which it gave rise, not only in the ranks of the ruling bureaucracy but also amongst the opposition.

In other words, on both sides of the political divide the active majority were not prepared to risk the possibility of annexation by the FRG. For this reason many individuals and groups on the Left in the GDR had to take on a critical approach to the existing system which, however, did not necessarily seek to destroy the system. As it states in the *Aufruf zur Einmischung in eigener Sache* (Appeal for intervention into our own affairs) of 12 September 1989, proclaimed by a group within the Protestant church: 'We want the socialist revolution, which has become stuck in the stage of nationalisation, to be carried forward into the future.'[53]

In this context, too, Land and Possekel quote the Berlin philosopher and politician M.O.

> For me it was probably the *Short History of the CPSU* [a Stalinist rewriting of the history of Bolshevism] which helped me make sense of everything. How did it happen? How did the GDR become so similar to the Soviet Union? I could see that the GDR wasn't like the Soviet Union in 1938, during the trials. Then the answer came to me; they had chucked it all away. Stalin and the Stalinists had distorted the revolution. There had been de-Stalinisation of course but what came out of it was a bureaucratic, petit-bourgeois, pathetic socialism which had nothing to do with revolutionary ideals. That strengthened me in my opposition to the regime in the GDR. I now had a historical explanation for my rejection.[54]

In this one quotation we can quite clearly see the critical element within GDR socialism proceeding from a recognition of both the terroristic

---

53. *Frankfurter Rundschau*, 3 October 1989, quoted in Manfred Behrend, 'Bürgerbewegungen in der DDR und danach – Aufstieg, Niedergang und Vermächtnis (1)', *Hintergrund* no. 3 (1997): pp. 16–35.
54. Land and Possekel, *Fremde Welten*, p. 21.

monumentalism of high Stalinism and the petty-bourgeois nature of the GDR under Ulbricht and Honecker towards a historical explanation explicitly designed to help M.O. maintain a commitment to the concept of socialism. This, it would seem to me, is a perfect example of Nietzsche's description of the psychological processes involved in the *Uses and Disadvantages of History*.

As a final example of the way in which this process takes place and how it is formed out of an original critical analysis and impetus (and how that process can come full circle back to criticism), it is necessary to examine briefly the status and role of Rosa Luxemburg for the Left in the GDR.

Luxemburg was one of the founding personalities of the German communist movement. Her theoretical work, as well as her practical intervention in the class struggle, was highly influential. The debate between her and the leaders of the Bolshevik revolution still figures as one of the most important discussions of the relative roles of the vanguard and the masses in socialist revolutions. Her approach was entirely critical and challenging of everything around her and her commitment to the ideas of the self-mobilisation of the working class still provides scope for discussion today and goes to the heart of any socialist project.

Her death at the hands of the Freikorps however, not only turned her into a martyr but also into someone whose political development was arrested and therefore, open to limitless reinterpretation. She was a sort of proto-Che Guevara for the German Left. With the Stalinisation of the KPD and the CPSU came the reification of Luxemburg's ideas. And yet with her reification came the deliberate suppression of her criticisms of the Leninist concept of the vanguard party. In this way she was killed off a second time in order to help kill off any possibility of the idea of socialism arising autonomously from below. However, what is monumentalist about this is the fact that, rather than simply being airbrushed out of history, she was celebrated and put into the pantheon of socialist martyrdom. Only her ideas were airbrushed.

In the later, antiquarian, GDR, she became even further weakened by the attempts to turn her into a mother figure (with Liebknecht as the father) who would look over and guard the GDR against all of its foes. Under Honecker, the annual march to her grave became a quasi-religious ritual and the ideas she actually stood for were buried even deeper under a layer of slogans and pieties.

She could also in turn transcend her own reification and be utilised by the critical Left, for example in their use of her slogan 'Freedom is always the freedom of the dissenter.' This simple phrase fundamentally challenged the monumentalists and antiquarians who had expropriated her image. That those using her words should be arrested and exiled from the GDR by those who used and distorted her image to bolster their own control of the state provides support for my thesis. The fact that the protesters disrupted the official Luxemburg/Liebknecht march shows how they too could see the process of symbolic reification which had taken place.

Based on the historical record there can be no doubt that had Luxemburg not been murdered in 1919, she would have thrown herself, with all her energy, into the struggle against Stalin. For his part, Stalin recognised that Luxemburg's political legacy posed an enormous threat. In 1931, as part of an intensified campaign against Trotsky and the Left opposition, Stalin wrote an open letter to the Soviet magazine *Proletskaja Revoljutsija*, in which he stated it would be entirely wrong to regard Trotsky and the Left opposition as a fraction inside the communist movement, and declared Luxemburg 'guilty', alongside Trotsky, of developing the internationalist perspective of 'permanent revolution'. Stalin's letter was quickly translated into German. Inside the KPD, Thälmann attacked the positions of Luxemburg and Trotsky. Stalin's critique of Luxemburg was taken over entirely by the leaders and theoreticians of the SED. Fred Oelßner's official party biography of Luxemburg of 1951 repeats virtually word for word Stalin's assessment:

> For no matter how great were Rosa Luxemburg's achievements in the cause of the working class, no matter how much we bow in awe before her life of struggle, no matter how much we love her for her untiring support of the workers we must not forget one thing: that her mistakes and errors – which led the working class down the wrong road – were great. Above all we must not close our eyes to the fact that it is not just about individual mistakes but about her whole system of thought (Luxemburgism).[55]

The Stalinist bureaucracy in the East was always ready to use parts of Rosa Luxemburg's critique of social democratic reformism in its polemics with the SPD, but in general the SED's relationship to Luxemburg's actual ideas remained hostile. And yet they could not ignore her. The main GDR publishing house was slow in compiling the collected works of Luxemburg, first published in 1970, and even then the edition was not complete. None of Luxemburg's valuable writings on the national question, which were mainly published in the organs of the Polish Social Democratic movement, were ever translated and published. This dichotomy was also recognised by many at the time in the GDR. Even the SED were not able to entirely erase her words from the collected works they published. As Wolf Biermann said, they were 'deeply buried but easy to find'.[56]

The reasons for the SED's ambivalence towards Luxemburg are obvious and yet the creation of a socialist mythology could not be pursued without her. For example, Steffen Mensching's poem about the reification of Rosa Luxemburg by the SED was one of the most discussed poems of

---

55. Fred Oelßner, *Rosa Luxemburg*, Berlin, 1951, p. 7.
56. From the Cologne concert in 1976, which led to the withdrawal of his citizenship.

the 1980s, attempting as it does to turn her back into a real person with real ideas.

> Whereas Becher had used a kind of mystical Christian imagery, not without erotic intensity, to signal his grief and elevate the revolutionary into a Christ-like martyr [monumentalism], and Bobrowski had taken up an image out of one of the prison letters of the lark as the soul of the heroine [antiquarian-ism], Mensching makes of her a very real and physical woman [critique].[57]

The PDS also has a relationship with Luxemburg which demonstrates all three of these positions. The hard-liners in the party can appeal to her as an enduring monument, the antiquarians see her as a comfortable identificatory figure and the critical members of the party see her ideas as a way of challenging the position of the former two groups as well as the leadership. The PDS has named its political foundation after her and a great debate was unleashed by the unauthorised placing of a statue of Luxemburg in the doorway of the PDS headquarters in Karl Liebknecht house in 1999.

This brief example of the monumental, antiquarian and critical approaches to Rosa Luxemburg shows how history and the interpretation of historical events and figures continue to play an important integrative role in intellectual and theoretical discussions within and around the PDS.[58] In forthcoming chapters I shall discuss the real function of these debates in greater detail and also demonstrate how historical interpreta-tion is central to the contemporary political stance of the PDS and the wider German Left.

---

57. Leeder, *Breaking Boundaries*, p. 127.
58. See, for example, W.F. Haug's introduction to Wolfgang Fritz Haug and Frigga Haug (eds) *Unterhaltungen über den Sozialismus nach seinem Verschwinden*, Berlin, 2002, p. 11.

Chapter 2

THE LONG COLD WAR AND THE SHORT POLITICAL CENTURY

*T*his chapter deals with the rise of the mass working class as a substantial political force in both East and West in the post-1917 period and traces developments through the first challenges to global welfarism in 1974 and the end of the social state in the 1990s. It was during this period that mass politics and democracy became accepted forms of political rule and that the interests of the mass parties of the working class were integrated, in one form or another, into the social project.

This period is the major focus within this chapter and the shift from monumentalism to antiquarianism, which has previously been analysed in political and ideological terms, will be further explained in the light of historical and economic shifts within this period. I take 1974 to be the significant turning-point within the short political century as this is the year in which the shift away from social policy based on mass political integration commenced. It is from this date onwards that we see an end to both the Butskellite consensus in the Western democracies and the Brezhnev social contract in the East. The collapse of communism, so often seen as something spontaneous and unpredictable, clearly had its roots in the global economic crisis of the 1970s. The second section of this chapter deals with the period in which the hegemony of politics is replaced by a return to the primacy of economic considerations in political planning and governmental decision making from 1974 onwards. This is a period which is only just being revealed in all its implications but I have outlined some of the current debates and located them within my theoretical framework.

The fundamental reason for this periodisation is primarily sociological and not merely conjunctural. The key to understanding the nature of the SED and the GDR and therefore the political background to both the *Wende* and its political consequences for the PDS is the position, size, consciousness and social formation of the working class and its role in the political and ideological struggles in the GDR. After dealing with the issues of Stalinism in the workers' movement I therefore intend to concentrate on the 'Honecker era' after 1971, the collapse of the GDR into a united Germany and the consequences of that for the various types of opposition. This latter period represents a central element in the dynamic of the 'systemically immanent' contradictions of a developed transitional bureaucracy and its rapid disappearance under the pressure of international restructuring between East and West. That is, change in the GDR will be presented as the articulation of social and international contradictions and not as an autonomous phenomenon.

On the 26 December 1934 Ernst Jünger wrote to Carl Schmitt that 'we are now in the twenty-second year of the World War only one third of which is now behind us'.[1] With this, Jünger was stating that the episodes and periods which we like to see as separate from each other and distinct in their nature actually represent a continuum. It was perhaps Jünger's inspiration which gave rise to Schmitt's concept of the 'global civil war'. Even as early as 1934 Jünger recognised that the twentieth century was likely to be, as Eric Hobsbawm indeed later contended, both short and extreme.[2] Jünger could see that the First World War was merely the opening shot in a long inter-systemic cold war of attrition which would last, just like the First World War itself, until both sides had exhausted themselves and one side could prevail.

He saw communism, fascism and capitalism as combatants in that war of attrition and, with his experience of combat, knew what effect attrition had on its participants: how the experience of struggle itself changed those engaged in the struggle, how daily survival supplanted the original aims of the war and how means and ends were mixed up until there was no significant difference between survival and victory. Philip Bobbit has taken up this idea in his book *The Shield of Achilles*.[3] One can very easily see how this became the *modus operandi* of the Eastern European states in the postwar period. That ineluctable military logic can also be applied to politics in the twentieth century. Post-communist parties everywhere, the PDS included, still function to some extent as rest-homes for old class warriors. Sloterdijk too has commented that 'the First World War can still be seen as an event in the history of metaphysics – in a certain way as a militaristic commentary on Nietzsche's "God is dead." The ego after the war is an inheritance without testament and is almost inevitably doomed to cynicism.'[4]

Now, in the twenty-first century, after the final end of Jünger's and Hobsbawm's century of extremes, we appear once again to be without

1. Ernst Jünger and Carl Schmitt, *Briefwechsel*, Stuttgart, 1999, p. 44.
2. Eric Hobsbawm, *Age of Extremes. The Short Twentieth Century 1914–1991*, London, 1995.
3. Philip Bobbit, *The Shield of Achilles. War, Peace and the Course of History*, London, 2002.
4. Peter Sloterdijk, *Critique of Cynical Reason*, London and New York, 1988, p. 386.

testament and doomed to cynicism. Almost all of the great motivating forces of human history have been emptied of their meaning. Communism, socialism, utopia, all of those words which once gave rise in many to an almost libidinal sense of hope,[5] now provoke merely disregard and incomprehension. At the other end of the spectrum, even neo-Nazism is but a thin and sickly copy of a powerful barbarism and nationalism, a mere shell of a concept filled with hopeless quixotic railing against globalisation and the end of stability.[6]

Nowhere is this more the case than in Germany and within Germany nowhere is this more so than with the history of the workers' movement. What Jünger was alluding to in his comments on the First World War was that the Russian revolution and the survival of the Soviet Union changed the basic motivating force behind social, foreign and military policy in the twentieth century. The First World War and the freezing of the Russian revolution actually stopped Marx's dynamic in its tracks. Therefore we can say that the Long Cold War started in 1917 and became the continuation of politics by other means until the collapse of communism. For the West, economic decision making now had to be carried out with an eye to the political situation of the working class. The rise of fascism, for example, can be seen as the political reaction to the challenge of Soviet socialism, not as some negative threat to civilisation as such, as maintained by Nolte,[7] but as a beacon of hope for many working-class voters in Germany and Italy.

Economic policies therefore began to flow to a great extent from political considerations and political considerations in turn flowed not from considerations of how to change things but of how to make them stay the same, how to ward off the challenge for radical change from below. This primacy of politics can therefore be seen to have had both a positive and a negative dimension. On the one hand, it offered a tendency towards potential stability for the vast majority of the working class. On the other hand, it also created a stagnated conservatism of power. As far as working-class politics themselves were concerned, all the great socialist millenarian ideologies of the nineteenth century, once they became the ideologies of governance, became de-ideologised methods of control. As such, 'ideology' became the pejorative term that Marx considered it to be, namely, false consciousness, rather than the positive force Lenin intended, i.e. as a politicisation of ideas.

With the emergence of a politicised and educated mass workers' movement and the triumph of the Russian revolution, leaders of capital were

5. See David Bathrick in Beth Linklater, 'GDR Studies in Britain', *Debatte* vol .7, No.2, 2000, p. 203.
6. Frederic Jameson, 'Globalization and Political Strategy', *New Left Review* no. 4, July/August, 2000, pp. 49–68.
7. Ernst Nolte, *Der europäische Bürgerkrieg 1917–1945. Nationalsozialismus und Bolschewismus*, Munich, 1997.

forced to consider not only how they were to get access to all the materials they needed elsewhere in the world but also how to treat their own domestic working class. For that reason, from 1917 to 1990 social policy was based not so much on the economic decisions alone but primarily on socio-political ones. The threat of radical reform or even revolution was a real one and made the adoption of social policies a political imperative. Class struggle and the fight for political rather than economic hegemony essentially drove the conflict of the interwar years. Economic policy was tailored to the political necessity of integrating rather than confronting the working class.

In the West that was the function of social democracy, Rooseveltian Keynesianism and fascism. In Stalin's Soviet Union and post-1945 Eastern Europe the motivation was similar. The bureaucratisation of socialism was designed to induce political quiescence either through terror, as in the years of the purges, or through integration, as in the postwar years, culminating in the Brezhnev social contract and the 'unity of economic and social policy' of the Honecker era.

In the postwar period, despite the fact that the world was divided into East and West along a political and geo-strategic fault line, and despite the fact that ideological propaganda played an important role on both sides, what actually took place was a gradual depoliticisation of working-class politics. The reification of ideology into anti-communism in the West and Marxist-Leninist catechisms in the East killed off mass political debate. On both sides of the Wall, real politics became a minority, élitist pursuit with only brief periods when there was limited participation by the working class in political unrest. On the whole the policy of integration had successfully removed the threat of widespread unrest and the traditional working class gradually disappeared from the political scene.

This was not only due to the structural changes in employment but is primarily linked to the demotivating experience of Stalinism and social democracy. The true content of the Brezhnev doctrine lay in the attempt to create a pact which could use force to prevent a repetition of 1956. This was accompanied by a Brezhnev contract, which, in return for political quiescence, guaranteed minimum standards of living. After 1968 this doctrine meant that 'reform communism' and the whole of Eastern Europe was 'Brezhnevised'. This was achieved at the cost of further political alienation between the party and the masses; an even greater reform deficit than in the Soviet Union and, above all, an even more acute economic crisis (as a result of the smaller nature of the national economies compared with that of the USSR) and a much greater degree of dependence on the West. This process was maintained for some fifteen years until Gorbachov was made General Secretary of the CPSU and introduced not only quantitatively but also qualitatively different reforms.

This was possible because after the slump of 1929 the world embarked on a long upward turn in economic prosperity which lasted well into the late 1960s. Despite all the short-term crises and booms and slumps, the overall picture was one of growing prosperity in the advanced world, both East and West. Real unrest, real change, only reappears on the scene after that prosperity begins to end and the long upward wave flattens out in the 1970s and begins to turn down, bringing with it mass unemployment and the pressure for a fundamental restructuring of the economy.

Thatcherism, Reaganism, neo-liberalism is the West's response to that crisis and eventually too the Soviet Union collapsed because of the same pressures. In many ways, once capitalism had defeated the Soviet Union, the world could return to the inter-imperialist rivalry of the nineteenth century, rather than maintaining the inter-systemic rivalry of the twentieth. The twentieth century therefore ended quasi-officially in the 1990s but its fate was already sealed in 1974 with the rise of what Bobbit has called the 'market-state'.[8]

The Primacy of Politics and the Long Cold War

A former CIA adviser, Chalmers Johnson, explained U.S. policy in the twentieth century in the following terms:

> *Johnson:* We know today that the National Security Agency was advising in the late 1940s that a global capitalist system under the leadership of the U.S.A. should be set up. That would be the only way to guarantee a peaceful world. As long as the Soviet Union existed in such a powerful form we were forced to be careful. But when Clinton came to power the imperial project was reinvigorated with the aim of casting the whole world in our image.
>
> *Spiegel:* In the nineteenth century that was called imperialism, now we call it globalisation.
>
> *Johnson:* Americans love inventing euphemisms. Free world, globalisation. That sounds nice and Latin and smacks of inevitability but it's all bullshit. Globalisation is an American Ideology.[9]

Chalmers Johnson may have put the case somewhat brutally and there is much to be criticised in his interview but it does summarise the history of the twentieth century very succinctly. Politics in the twentieth century was determined not primarily by the existence of the Soviet Union but by the power and influence of an organised mass industrial working class in both East and West. What Johnson fails to recognise in this interview is that the working class was as strong in the West as the bureaucracy was in the East and that concessions had to be made and care taken with regard to the domestic working class as well as the USSR.

8.   Bobbit, *The Shield of Achilles*, p. xxvi.
9.   Chalmers Johnson 'Die Rolle eines Ersatz-Rom', *Der Speigel*, 45/2000, 254.

Mathias Greffrath, writing in *Die Zeit*, maintains that it was the European social state which brought about the end of communism, although how it did this is not really explained.

> It was the European social state which robbed communism of its legitimacy. Its demise should have marked the moment of Europe's triumph but since the fall of the Wall the European nations have subordinated themselves to globalisation and the rules for that were written under the auspices of the 'Washington Consensus' of 1989 by the U.S.A. Since then in Europe too we have seen tax cuts and privatisations of all the things which used to belong to the people – transport systems, the media, culture. Even the ultra-liberal *Economist* sighs: 'What is Europe for if it is just going to be a copy of the U.S.A?'[10]

This would seem to be a mixture of sober analysis and wishful thinking. On the one hand he acknowledges that the security of the welfare state has been broken down by the ravages of globalisation, but on the other hand, he wishes it to play a central role in European politics. However, the social state in Europe was no more able to avoid the effects of neoliberalism on a global scale than was the Soviet Union and they were both brought into crisis in similar ways. Bobbit has recognised this trend as well when he states that: 'A great epochal war has just ended. The various competing systems of contemporary nation-state (fascism, communism, parliamentarism) that fought that war all took their legitimacy from the promise to better the material welfare of their citizens. The market-state offers a different covenant: it will maximise the opportunity of its people.'[11]

Thus the end of Fordism, the end of the Cold War, and the collapse of communism and the welfare state as well as the onset of globalisation are all closely linked phenomena determined by, but also determining, economic developments. In an interview the author conducted with Gregor Gysi, the issue of the primacy of politics was directly addressed:

> PT: Is that what you meant when you once said that the job of the left was to re-establish the primacy of politics over economics and does that mean that the PDS is now the only real **political** party in Germany, the others all having become economic parties, i.e. subservient to economic interests?

> GG: I believe that the primacy of politics is the precondition for the establishment of democratic structures and the ability of people to intervene in their own affairs. If economic interests continue to prevail over those of politics then power remains anonymous and undemocratic because it is not elected from below but is located in the boardrooms of the big companies and politics is about carrying out the decisions made there. The primacy of politics means, above all, creating a regulatory capacity even over economics, over international financial and speculative markets, over the world economy and trade and exchange on a more just basis than today. That is the primacy of politics because in politics

10. Mathias Greffrath, 'Weder Dschungel noch Zoo. Nur in der Verteidigung des Sozialstaates kann Europa seine politische Identität finden', *Die Zeit* 9 November 2000, p. 13.
11. Bobbit, *The Shield of Achilles*, p. xxvi.

people have choices and that is where democracy is rooted and not in the board-room. That is why the question of the primacy of politics is of central importance for the left if it wants to influence social developments.[12]

During the nineteenth and early twentieth centuries the aim of the workers' movement was to arrive at a critique of the political economy of capitalism in which liberationist politics would conquer and subordi-nate economic primacy to social imperatives. People everywhere were to be liberated from the realm of necessity into the realm of freedom. The term social democracy was coined precisely to express this idea that society, in other words the majority working class, should not only be granted political influence but should exercise social control over produc-tion, distribution and exchange. The nineteenth century was one dominated by the great empires' struggle for dominance and access to resources. However, the struggle they engaged in was inter-imperialist and not inter-systemic. It was the struggle of similar systems working through the medium of national formation for economic hegemony. However, the ideological background to the struggle was relatively weak and economics reigned supreme. Marketisation and globalisation in the form described by Marx were the main driving forces. Capitalism would bring down the Chinese walls of feudalism and nationalist particularism and the great capitalist enterprises represented the battering rams of the market. Marx saw this entirely as an economic struggle, however, out of which political consequences would flow. For him the great capitalist states merely represented social organisations which all would be forced, whatever their national peculiarities, to follow.

The tragedy of the twentieth century is that in a very limited sense the workers' movement both succeeded and failed. The powerful economic intentions behind social democracy forced the advanced states in the West to make political concessions in order to ward off the more radical demands of the workers' movement. In this way the short twentieth century did indeed become the workers' century, but in a half-finished form. For the first time in history the working class became integrated into political considerations and gained representation and influence. However, rather than the direct democracy of producers and consumers envisaged by Marx, what occurred was the vicarious exercise of workers' power through social democratic parties which were increasingly satis-fied with the political gains made.

As a result, the revolutionary Left became highly critical of what was seen as the democratic camouflage of 'bourgeois parliamentary cretinism' (Lenin). This also meant that their approach to questions of state power became radically economistic. The social revolution in the economic base became more important than the pursuit of political freedoms. The two

12. Peter Thompson 'The Primacy of Politics – Interview with Gregor Gysi', *Debatte* vol. 3/ no.1, 2002, pp. 25–31.

wings of the workers' movement mirrored each other in that the reformist wing elevated democratic demands over socio-economic ones and the revolutionary wing elevated the primacy of economic transformation over democratic demands.

Both of these roads, resulting from the split in the workers' movement, were equally aberrant and each led to their own forms of monumentalism. The SPD's limited political influence in the West reified short-term political imperatives at the cost of the goal of socialism. The reality of social democratic politics turned from critique to a monumentalism in which – in the words of Eduard Bernstein – 'the movement became everything and the goal nothing'.[13] Within the confines of absolute bureaucratic rule in the East, on the other hand, the goal became everything and the means of achieving it merely a tactical consideration. Marx, Engels, Lenin, Luxemburg, Liebknecht, Kautsky etc. all became the reified monuments to a false consciousness of social democratic or communist power rather than tools in the hands of those determined to undermine power.

The tragedy of the division of the German workers' movement was not then primarily one of the weight of numbers or of political influence but the fact that the objective and the subjective, the economic and the political, the base and the superstructure, the theoretical and the practical elements of the dialectic of socialist development became divorced from each other. That this political division was translated into a geographical one after 1945 simply compounded the problem. Social democracy in the West gradually abandoned any desire to bring about a fundamental change in the economic base of society and communism in the East withdrew into an even more vulgar economistic position in which the mere existence of the socialised means of production was seen as the attainment of socialism *per se* and democratic demands as counter-revolutionary. It was the inflexibility which arose from these attitudes towards economic policy which led to the collapse of communism, not the positive example of the Western social state. The Western social state existed as a political necessity in the time of inter-systemic rivalry and was at best a halfway house to socialism. This is what is meant here by the political century: the massification of politics and the subordination of market imperialism to social inclusivity. What must be emphasised here, however, is that this transition to inclusivity was something forced upon the rulers in both East and West by the sheer specific weight of the industrial working class and its central role in the productive process.

13. It is interesting to note here how André Brie remarked recently in an interview with *Neues Deutschland* (ND): 'It is terrible to see how the old ideological enmities of the GDR live on and even worse to see the intellectual richness of Bernstein's work lying fallow...' ND, 13 February 1999. This statement in itself unleashed a storm of debate about the nature of the PDS leadership carried out in the pages of *Junge Welt* between Gregor Gysi and Winfried Wolf, see http://www.jungewelt.de/1999/03–09/014.shtml

By 1974 the political agenda moved away from the integration of the working classes and their parties in West and East towards the resumption of economic prioritisation from above against the interest of the workers. This took place in both power blocs but the consequences for the rule of the bureaucracy in the Soviet bloc are immeasurably greater. There is no contradiction here in describing the Soviet bloc's policies as essentially economistic and yet locating them in an essentially political century, as the politics pursued in that bloc were designed merely to consolidate power on the basis of transformed property relations. The political century is, therefore, one of deformed, static and reified politics.

The period after 1974 has seen increasing trends towards the globalisation of production, distribution and exchange and represents the continuation of the process outlined by Marx in the *Communist Manifesto*. The objective economic trend is towards a globalisation and internationalisation of production and away from national productive units. Ideologically, too, an apparently depoliticised pragmatism holds sway and the dominant political debate is about the degree of control which nation states can have over their own societies and economies. Behind the scenes, however, great ideological movements are taking place around such economic issues as the role of the WTO, GATT and NAFTA[14] and the way in which economic priorities are now being enshrined in international trade agreements. These agreements are designed to make it illegal for any nation state to prevent free international trade in favour of the social provision of public services in areas such as transport and health. All of these agreements are also designed to return the world to the position which prevailed before 1917. They are also explicitly greeted as such.

Having outlined the major trends and turning points in the twentieth century, the first task here is to demonstrate how the Long Cold War defined and determined politics in Germany in the twentieth century. As we have seen, monumentalism lasted from the late 1920s until the late 1950s in both East and West. These were the years of high Stalinism in the East and reformist social democracy in the West. In both sectors of the bipolar world, socialist ideologies were reduced to the creation of monumental dogmas commanding absolute loyalty. In Germany itself, this monumentalism was the main reason behind the inability of the workers' parties to work together to effectively combat the real dangers arising from the fundamental instability of the economics of capitalism. The political loyalty of the SPD to the Weimar Republic and the subservience of the KPD to Stalin's political degeneration of the communist ideal into the Greater Russian chauvinism of socialism in one country helped fascism to victory in Europe.

14. See, for example, Jeanne Rehberg, *WTO/GATT Research*
   http://www.llrx.com/features/wto.htm#WTO/GATT Legal Instruments

After the Second World War, the same form of monumentalism continued but was in turn frozen into a geopolitical split in which Germany again played a central role. West Germany's social democrats reluctantly accepted political subservience to the new masters in Washington and East Germany's communists, less reluctantly, to the strategic exigencies of Moscow's hegemony. The transitional period between monumentalism and antiquarianism lasted for around ten years between 1945 and the mid to late 1950s. These were the years of deep uncertainty about relations between East and West in Germany and the rest of the world.

During this transitional period, politics in the GDR were consumed with deep ideological schisms and debates about how to achieve a united socialist Germany. From Ackermann's 'German path to socialism' to the Berija-Zaisser-Herrnstadt and the Schirdewan-Wollweber-Harich groups which emerged in the conflicts with Ulbricht about Germany and socialism, ideological debates raged about how to overcome division. The uprising of 1953 was led by communists and social democrats in the East who sought to link up with their comrades in the West in order to liberate both from their geopolitical masters.[15] The SED's disciplinary measures after the 17 June were carried out predominantly against millions of its own members and supporters who had sought to bring about the workers' unity which had been missing in Weimar.

In the West, too, social democracy was fighting the same battles. From Schumacher's attack on Adenauer as the 'Allied Chancellor' in 1949 through to the SPD's *Deustchlandplan* of 1959, there was still a dialectical desire to achieve workers' unity through German unity and vice versa. The SPD's adoption of the *Godesberg Program* in late 1959 and the SED's acceptance of the need to abandon any hopes of German unity, culminating in the building of the Berlin Wall in August 1961, were two sides of the same coin. Both had to accept that the desire to create socialism in any form which would be recognisable to socialists had to be (at best) postponed until the division of the world into East and West came to an end.

It is that recognition which marks the end of the monumentalist period of socialist ideologies and the adoption of the second period: namely, that of antiquarianism in which socialism itself becomes an empty phrase, devoid of any real content and merely about acquiescence and capitulation to the reality of power. In other words, this meant the adoption of neo-Stalinism in the East and 'NATO social democracy' in the West. In true Hegelian form, however, monumentalism, the period in which mass power still had to be consolidated, had contained within it elements of criticism and real ideological struggle and antiquarianism had contained residual elements of monumentalism in the form of Marxist-Leninist catechisms and lip-service to socialism. In both periods there was an absence

15. See, for example, Günter Minnerup, 'The Bundesrepublik Today', *New Left Review* no. 99, 1976, pp. 3–46.

of effective criticism and an emphasis on the bureaucratic ideology of consolidated power. The ideologies which existed were primarily designed to justify the adoption of the wrong path. That is, after all, what real existing socialism means: non-existent socialism.

The problem for both those who were supporters of the Stalinist system, whatever their personal worries, and those who were vehement opponents of it, is that the laws of development and forms of movement in social and political conflict in the post-capitalist societies were, for clearly political reasons, only ever investigated in relatively rudimentary form. This is particularly the case for those post-capitalist societies which had a developed social structure comparable to that of the capitalist industrial world, such as the GDR. This is not merely of academic and historical interest, however. Post-reunification Germany remains a divided country not only because of the modalities of transition and the economic dislocation created in both the ex-GDR and the old West German state, but also because the social transformation which occurred in the GDR before 1989 continues to affect political relationships within Germany to this day.

Again, the role of the PDS can only be understood properly, rather than in the rhetorical form it takes today, when these socio-historical factors are understood. The revolution of 1989/90 in the GDR saw the various factions within the SED thrown into considerable confusion. What we find is that many of the careerist SED members in the party and state apparatuses ended up in the forefront of the movement for bourgeois restoration while many, in sociological terms, petty-bourgeois or even bourgeois elements opposed reunification alongside those members of the SED who remained committed to the ideals of socialism.

However, the form of socialism they remained committed to was one which was fatally hampered by its degeneration into Stalinist power politics. As we have seen, Stalinism is characterised by the fact that social and economic decisions are taken for overwhelmingly political reasons to do with the system of bureaucratic control and not to increase labour productivity in order to liberate the workers from the 'yoke of labour', the fundamental *raison d'être* of a socialist economy. The bureaucracy was always faced with this central contradiction of how to raise labour productivity. It could only be done in three ways, all of which were tried at some point: firstly, through ideological commitment; secondly, through terror and discipline; and, thirdly, through marketisation and technological investment.

All of these courses bring with them considerable problems and all three were attempted to varying degrees in the GDR. An ideological commitment to working harder will work as long as those doing the work feel that the future they are building is worthwhile. The *Aufbaugeneration* of the first years of the GDR still had, despite all their doubts about Stalinism, an ideological commitment to the creation of a socialist state.

Under Stalin after the great purges, this was certainly not the case for many, and the ideological hope which many communist workers and intellectuals demonstrated in the first years of the GDR was wasted by the bureaucracy as it became clear that its own survival and the unconditional defence of its Soviet equivalent were the only measure of success.

This leads to the use of discipline and outright terror, the use of slave labour, gulags, increased work norms and the use of secret police methods, etc. The disadvantages of this system are obvious and well documented. The Stakhanovite movement in Eastern Europe tended to combine both of these options. On the one hand, it was a deliberately propagandistic and ideological struggle, but those who refused to follow the lead were very quickly accused of sabotage and treated harshly accordingly.

When these methods failed, then the party tended to turn to marketisation and technological renewal. These, however, brought with them a tendency towards creating instability and insecurity amongst the working class, who, they were told, were living in workers' states. The supposed advantages of liberalisation therefore had to be accompanied by expensive subsidisation of working-class life. The costs of this subsidisation more than outstripped any productivity gains from liberalisation. Indeed, productivity actually fell at some points because the security of employment led to an inbuilt inefficiency, in which, in order to fulfil the plan targets, requirements of raw materials and labour power were overemphasised and potential output was underplayed. As no one could be sacked for these distortions, corruption and inefficiency rather than increased labour productivity resulted.

It is for this combination of reasons that we can say that in Eastern Europe there was neither capitalism nor socialism but that the central concern of the party was to mobilise the working class in the name of the working class. Sebastian Gerhardt, for example, describes the Eastern European economies as 'nominally socialist'.[16] Essentially this means that the problems of both society and economy in the GDR emanated not, as is often maintained, from the socialised ownership of the means of production, but from the de-socialised relations of political control and decision making over the economy. Gerhardt says of the Soviet Politburo, for example: 'the function of the Politbureaucracy was reduced to that of a mobilising agency which had very little to do with the development of policy but which was essential in its implementation'.[17] If this was the case in the Soviet Union, which had at least had its own revolution, then it was much more so in the GDR, where the state's policies were illegitimate in domestic terms, but were also imposed from outside by Soviet decree.

16. Sebastian Gerhardt *Politbürokratie und Hebelwirtschaft in der DDR. Zur Kritik einer moralischen Ökonomie*, Berlin, 1997.
17. Ibid., p. 7.

Where I disagree with Gerhardt, however, is in his contention that Stalinism ended in 1953.[18] Although his is a well-presented case, it ignores the fact that Stalinism under Stalin also underwent all sorts of tactical swerves and implemented all sorts of measures to secure the position of the bureaucracy. Perhaps a good compromise would be to speak of the post-1953 period as one of neo-Stalinist or weak Stalinist rule. However, I believe that the definition of Stalinism should not lie so much in an identification of its methods but in its socio-political role as a tool of the bureaucracy. It is, after all, by its very nature impossible for Stalinism to democratise itself, for to do so would, in the context of the dialectic of quantity into quality and as the Gorbachov reforms showed, lead to its own demise. When Gerhardt quotes Bernd Gehrke's point that the GDR was not Stalinist because it did not have the potential to introduce 'terror like that of the Third Reich or the Soviet Union'[19] at will, he ignores the fact that there were no formal institutions in force which could have prevented its introduction if they had wanted to try it. When it came to 1989, as Martin Koch points out, the state still had 272,000 men and women under arms, none of whom had gone over the to the opposition and 'no one knew how a weakened SED leadership would react'.[20] That it would not have worked because the people would not have stood for it is questionable. The party had called for increased battle readiness and Krenz had been the one sent to Beijing to congratulate the Communist Party there for their 'decisive action' in Tienanmen Square. As Koch points out, nobody knew whether he would be the 'communist Noske' or not.

However, the key to understanding the political dynamic of Eastern Europe and the GDR lies not in some fundamental antagonism between the working class and communism but in the question of why the party and state leaderships undertook certain reforms which were bound to affect the population negatively, apparently in full recognition of the risks involved.

Here we come up against the reverse side of the coin of the maturation of the East European societies beyond their post-revolutionary stage. The completion of the transformation process, although positive for the bureaucracy in bringing about the neutralisation of internal and external restorationist forces, brought with it new and different problems. Economically, the inherent advantages of the planned economy in the process of 'primitive accumulation' and extensive industrialisation were coming to an end. Since the end of the 1960s, the annual growth rates in the COMECON countries showed an unstoppable tendency to fall. Although I would question the explanation he gives for it, Kurt Biedenkopf draws attention to this fact in his address to the World Bank group:

18. Ibid., p. 8.
19. Ibid., p. 9.
20. Martin Koch, 'Kein kommunistischer Noske' *ND* 7 November 1998, p. 15.

In the first 10 years [after 1949], growth rates were somewhat the same, and development of the Germanies was also somewhat the same, and then the East was falling back, and finally stagnating in real development. The main reason for this ... is that centrally planned economies can only manage a certain level of complexity, and as you develop an economy, with the increasing perform-ance of your economy, complexity increases. In other words, if you want to increase the performance of your economy, of your administration, of your division of labor, you have got to be able to manage increasing complexities. Centrally planned bureaucracies cannot do this, and as a consequence, in the late 1960s, early 1970s, the economic development in the GDR began to stag-nate.[21]

Growth rates and share of world trade in the 1960s are shown by World Bank statistics to have been falling or at best stagnating. By the 1960s, average growth rates had begun to decline and with this the growth of living standards. In the period 1951–1960, the growth of industrial production was more than 10 per cent and the average for the decade was around 12 per cent per year. But, in 1963 and 1964, officially claimed industrial growth rates fell below 8 per cent, the lowest peacetime figures except 1933.[22]

Table 2.1. Growth Rates in Eastern Europe and the Soviet Union

Growth rates:	1950–55	1955–60	1960–65	1965–70
USSR	11.3%	9.2%	6.3%	4.0%
Czech	8.0%	7.1%	1.8%	3.4%
Poland	8.6%	6.6%	5.9%	6.7%
Bulgaria	12.2%	9.7%	6.5%	4.5%

This trend continued until, by 1979, GDP in the Soviet Union grew by only 3.6 per cent. The annual average increase in labour productivity was still rising in the 1960s and early 1970s. But from 1975 to 1980, this slumped to 3.4 per cent and by 1982 it was 2.5 per cent per year. In 1979, GNP grew by a mere 0.9 per cent, and in 1980 by 1.5 per cent.[23]

At the same time, the pressure to move towards very expensive tech-nological innovation and investment grew enormously. In the military sector, this was because of the need to maintain parity with the West, and in the civil sector because of the third technological revolution (microprocessors, the automation of production processes and informa-tion technology), which was increasingly dominating the world markets. As 'developed' societies which were still relatively backward and which

---

21. Kurt Biedenkopf, 'The Transition Process in Germany and Its Relevance for Europe', http://www.worldbank.org/wbi/lectures/bieden-text.html.
22. World Bank, *World Development Report*, 1981, p. 135. Quoted by Ted Grant, 'Russia: From Revolution to Counterrevolution', http://easyweb.easynet.co.uk/ ~ socappeal/ russia/part6.html
23. Ibid.

had concentrated on military and industrial development, the Eastern Bloc countries possessed neither the organisational preconditions nor the material resources necessary for keeping up with the West in the long term. The longer the attempt to keep up with the West under the old system of production, the more the strategic sectors had to be privileged over the production of consumer goods. In purely economic terms, the fundamental problem for the post-capitalist states was the inability to raise the level of labour productivity and to mobilise social resources for a great technological leap forward. This demonstrates a further negative consequence of the maturity of the antiquarian bureaucratic societies.

Under Stalin during the period of monumentalism, it had indeed been possible, through the extensive exploitation of resources and the use of Stakhanovite labour methods and simple material incentives, to raise the level of labour productivity. However, by the 1970s and 1980s the mobilisation of the population via these ideological and material methods was no longer possible. In the Soviet Union and Eastern Europe, the generation of *Altkommunisten*, who, because of their ideological commitment and self-motivation, were prepared to play the role of the model worker and leader of work brigades, had almost completely died out. More important, though, is the fact that the material incentives in the form of bonuses and socialist competition which characterised the Brezhnev period had lost their effectiveness in two ways: firstly, because the monetary reward far outstripped the availability of goods and, secondly, because the collectives always found ways of obtaining these bonuses without actually improving the level of productivity.

In the period of *détente* between the blocs, as strategic parity coincided with a capitalist boom, the Brezhnev leadership put all their energies into reducing the cost of strategic arms spending by concluding arms-control treaties with the West and by rapidly expanding trade in order to earn the hard currency necessary for investment in new technologies. By the end of the 1970s, these intentions came up against unexpected limitations resulting from a combination of factors:

1. The crisis in the capitalist world led to a contraction of export markets.
2. Rising interest rates and energy prices drastically increased the mountains of debt accrued by the state banks.
3. The U.S.A. used the 'second cold war'[24] to increase the technological level of strategic rearmament to a level with which they knew the USSR could not compete.
4. The COCOM rules were also introduced in order to deny the Soviet Union access to strategically important technology.

The country which suffered most from these developments was Poland, which, under Gierek, had gone furthest in modernising the economy on

24. See Fred Halliday, *The Making of the Second Cold War*, London, 1983.

the basis of exports to and credits from the West, but Hungary, Romania and Czechoslovakia were almost as badly hit. Only the Soviet Union, because of the immense size of its internal market, and the GDR, because of its privileged connections with the West via West Germany, could survive this setback without too many symptoms of crisis. But even they were eventually to face exactly the same problems as the rest of Eastern Europe. At base, these problems rested on the tension between promoting economic efficiency and yet maintaining the political quiescence of the working class.

The relationship to the working class was characterised, after Khrushchev's de-Stalinisation process, by a sort of informal social contract. This meant that the primary instrument of social control was no longer the use of open force or ideological indoctrination as in the monumentalist period, but a combination of material incentives and social security. Politically this meant that the passivity of the workers and their readiness to accept the absence of elementary democratic rights was purchased via the guarantee of constantly rising levels of consumption and a secure job. Economically, it meant changing the means of improving labour productivity from one based on collective fear to one based on material competition between individuals and small-scale work brigades. Simultaneously, the reins in the area of culture and the use of free time were partially loosened and the party and state allowed a relatively liberal attitude to people's spare-time activities as long as they conformed in the workplace. What the statistics above clearly demonstrate, though, is that the economic preconditions for this policy were largely missing. Social stability and mass subsidisation of employment and consumption assume constant and high growth rates. Keynesianism in the West was predicated upon this assumption and the welfare dictatorship of the East far more so.

In judging the relationship between the bureaucracy and the workers, it should not be overlooked that the period between 1956 and the late 1970s was a period in which the great majority of Soviet and Eastern European workers enjoyed unprecedented improvements in their standard of living. We should not be surprised, therefore, that between those dates there was not one single example of serious, economically motivated rebellion by the working class. The dissident intellectuals, who benefited from the policy of cultural liberalisation, could therefore be isolated from the working class and their political impact strictly limited. In the GDR this change is clearly evident.

In the initial monumentalist and transitional periods, the working class played a central role in social conflict. There were many elements of the old social democratic and communist traditions in Germany who were still committed to the original ideals of socialism and who were prepared to challenge the regime on the basis of those ideals. The highly ideological propaganda statements about the GDR on the part of the regime were taken at face value and the discrepancy between promise and reality was, for the workers, very clear. After the 1953 uprising, and particularly after the replacement of Khrushchev with Brezhnev, Ulbricht and Honecker were concerned not to do anything to antagonise the working class again. In doing so, however, it was necessary to downplay the ideological imperatives of the monumentalist period and replace them with the establishment of social stability which characterises the antiquarian period.

The history of the Soviet bloc shows that any analysis of the GDR which concerns itself exclusively with mass revolt from below is over-simplistic. In addition to an analysis of the opposition's political and organisational forms, the role of intellectuals and other dissident groups as well as the role of the lower party cadres and ordinary members of the ruling parties, it is always necessary to consider the levels of party and state leadership and the international relationship within the Eastern Bloc and between East and West. It is therefore necessary to reject the concept that bureaucratic rule was ever going to be swept away in some cataclysmic and spontaneous uprising of the masses. This interpretation ignores the central importance of the role of the bureaucracy itself in its own downfall.

The idea that the revolution in the Eastern Bloc came essentially from below can be found on the Right as well as the Left and, despite all their ideological differences, is rooted in some common assumptions. Both underestimate the social roots of the existing bureaucracies and overestimate the alleged social consensus about what was to replace the bureaucracy. The debate continues to this day, with reformed communist parties maintaining their positions in Eastern Europe and combining the practice of market reforms with the rhetoric of social solidarity. This continues to confuse many commentators and in the ex-GDR led the continuing strength of the PDS to be underestimated.

The general view in the West was that the old ruling Stalinist structures were seen as thoroughly rotten, socially completely isolated and therefore ripe for complete collapse at any moment. They would be replaced with either capitalist democracy or 'true socialism', which, according to political stance, was what the people were supposedly striving for. The reality of the situation is considerably more complex. The bureaucratic regime represented not only a specific totalitarian political order but also an economic and social order which was experienced as a repressive yoke but which also structured the daily lives of people in a positive way.

The party leaderships in the satellite states formed after 1945 were in no way mere Stalinist puppets. Within them existed many national communist currents which had their own ideas about the route their own countries should take to socialism. After Stalin's death, as the struggle for succession was won by those pushing for de-Stalinisation, these national communist currents experienced a degree of rehabilitation, which eventually led to deep political crisis, culminating in the events in Hungary and Poland in 1956. The Soviet Union was able to reassert control through direct military intervention in Hungary or a combination of threats and concessions in Poland, but the old monolithic nature of the world communist movement could not be re-established. Only in the GDR was this process effectively halted, with the bringing into line of the leadership after the expulsion and disciplining of national communist oppositionists, such as Zaisser, Herrnstadt, Schirdewan, Wollweber, Harich and Janka in the years 1953–1957.

Again, the reasons for this are to be found in the international situation prevailing at that time. Relative relaxation in Eastern Europe had to be based on an absolute stability in East–West relations. The GDR, as the front line of the Soviet bloc, was made to pay the price for a new Soviet *modus operandi* with the West. Tito's departure from the socialist camp (retrospectively sanctioned by Khrushchev in 1956) had opened up a new era of polycentrism in Europe, which found its most spectacular expressions in Albanian Maoism, Ceaucescu's Romania and the drifting off of the Western Communist Parties into 'Eurocommunism'. Less spectacularly, though just as significantly, in every other state in the Soviet bloc national communist currents found a voice, apart from in the GDR, where the development of an antiquarian 'GDR nationalism' at the behest of the Soviet leadership effectively silenced the limited national communist traditions within the SED.

In this context the Prague Spring of 1968 represented, until Gorbachov's programme of perestroika and glasnost, the most extreme experiment in controlled de-Stalinisation from above. It was tolerated by Moscow at first because of the vital need to improve the Czech economy, but the reform movement drifted out of control at the point where the Dubček leadership's economic and technocratic reforms, designed to rectify the economic and social crisis created under Novotny and to reverse the trend towards falling growth rates, developed into a dynamic towards full democratisation.

Later, Gorbachov sought to learn from the experience of Czechoslovakia in 1968 by combining technocratic and democratic reforms (perestroika and glasnost) from the very beginning, but the end result was just as disastrous for the party, if not the bureaucracy. In 1968 the invasion of Warsaw Pact troops set clear limits on the reform communist project in Eastern Europe: economic reforms and ideological independence, yes; but political pluralism and independence of the masses, no. Instead, Brezhnev gave the green light to an attempt to solve economic and social problems through a policy of *détente* which would open the gates to Western technology, management techniques, capital investment and hard currency. However, this social contract combined with an opening up to the West had two serious long-term consequences for the bureaucracy:

Firstly, it was enormously expensive, as a result of the massive subsidisation of consumer prices which, in the case of basic goods, remained unchanged for over twenty years. This not only overburdened the state budget but distorted the price structure and made later economic reforms much more difficult. Secondly, the individualisation of competition in the workplace was ineffective because there was a basic lack of consumer goods to spend extra money on and also because there was no threat of unemployment to act as a disciplining force. Ted Grant, in a section of glowing praise for the conditions in the Soviet Union under Brezhnev, describes life thus:

> The growth in living standards was achieved with virtually no inflation. Above all, the prices of basic necessities were kept low. Bread was so cheap that the peasants would feed it to their livestock instead of grain. A particularly important gain was low rents. Whereas a worker in the West spends anything between a third and a half of his wage on rent, the situation in the USSR was totally different. Out of a 200 rouble monthly wage, only 10 roubles a month went on rent, and this included hot water, central heating, and, at least in Moscow, free local phone calls. There was a completely free education and health service, no unemployment and a month's free holiday at resorts run by the trade unions. The Soviet Union probably had the best public transport system in the world, with extremely low fares – five kopecks for any distance in Moscow, for example.[25]

All of this may be true, but it had to be paid for out of an economic base which, we have already seen, was rapidly declining. The lack of unemployment and the resulting strength of the working class, combined with the political necessity for massive subsidisation, were actually amongst the main reasons for the collapse of the system in the end. The introduction of new labour-saving technology under the auspices of the 'scientific-technical revolution' did not lead to the expected increases in productivity and the liberalisation of labour power. The Polish mass strikes against price rises in 1970 and 1976 showed quite clearly that under the Brezhnev social contract the workers had effectively been given a right of veto over economic policy.

For Gierek, Honecker and Kadar, who followed this course most enthusiastically (and in the long term for the USSR itself), it brought new problems of economic dependence on the Western world and further exposure to subversive ideological influences, which in turn helped to create new forms of opposition movements and a new round of conflicts of interest within the bureaucracy. This was particularly the case for the GDR, of course, with its close links with West Germany. The opposition in the last period in the GDR became increasingly divorced from the

25. Grant, 'Russia: From Revolution to Counterrevolution'.

workers and their interests and took many of the political and ideological cues from the post-materialist generation in West Germany. This meant that the bureaucracy tended to obscure its own inability to solve the real objective problems of economic inefficiency with workerist attacks on the opposition. In other words, the bureaucracy could not break the contract with the workers without risking serious unrest and deep political crisis and the linking of the working class with the new anti-communist intellectual layer would prove an explosive mixture. The year 1980/81 greatly emphasised this lesson and it is significant that even with the smashing of Solidarnosć and the introduction of martial law, the Jaruzelski leadership was still not able to introduce price rises, wage reductions or to liberalise labour power and that even the official unions, invented by the regime as a form of ersatz-Solidarnosć, were not prepared to go along with such reforms. In this sense at least, the Eastern Bloc states really were 'workers' states', in that the classical bourgeois methods of overcoming economic crisis by making the working class pay via inflation or unemployment – as had happened in the West – were politically impossible.

It was not state ownership of the means of production, economic planning and the absence of class barriers in access to education and social security *per se* which were the targets of popular scorn and mobilisation, but the bureaucracy's mismanagement and corruption of those institutions. The advantages of the old economic and social order were also not merely abstract concepts for broad layers of the working population of Eastern Europe, but also provided real material benefits and improvements. The resistance to perestroika and economic reforms which were based on an austerity programme had very contradictory effects. On the one hand, they were undertaken against a working class which was already demoralised and politically atomised and it was clear to the vast majority that in material terms they were a step backwards for their living standards and conditions. The introduction of unemployment and the law of value was not widely welcomed in the USSR.[26] On the other hand, however, because it was the party which was introducing these capitalist reform measures, the opposition to the reforms was undertaken against the party rather than the neo-liberal nature of the reforms. The reforms and their consequences were seen not as a direct corollary of the party's adoption of ever greater neo-liberal methods of reward and distribution but of its inherent inability to run society in any way. Therefore, when the revolutions came, they swept away the party and communism – which were not the fundamental cause of the problems – and left behind the austerity and increasingly bourgeois nature of the party's economic programmes – which were.

26. This is the reason why Gorbachov, the initiator and instigator of those reforms, remains perhaps the most hated figure in Russia today.

The situation was very different in times of relative stability such as under the antiquarian rule of Erich Honecker. The influence of critical party cadres in these conditions is weak because in normal times political criticism was not permitted and the party was able to present itself to the people as a monolithic institution. Without ideological reference points and uncontrolled organisational free space, the masses remained atomised and unable to take the political initiative. Even when there was widespread dissatisfaction, it was expressed passively in things such as a lower level of commitment at work, a retreat from social activity into family life, consumerism, alcoholism, etc. Only the church offered a limited opportunity for overcoming social isolation. Individual protest or resistance was rare as it usually only led to further social isolation or even criminalisation.[27]

Criticism, dissent and opposition existing under these conditions were necessarily limited to certain specific social layers. In particular these were found in the academic, artistic and philosophical institutions, the universities, the media and the churches, and within various national minorities, underground and youth movements. These groups were therefore not necessarily representative of the consciousness of the wider society. Many of their ideological characteristics and practical forms of articulation reflected the milieu-related specificities of their existence: in particular in that they were preoccupied with reflection on and contemplation of their circumstances and, in contradistinction to real mass movements, only rarely agitated for concrete practical goals. Within these milieux – which were less affected by general social relations of power than by their own specific problems and, often coincidental, personal contacts and ideological references – the weight of religious, bourgeois, foreign but also oppositional Marxist, anarchistic and other minority interests was much greater than in society as a whole.

This role as non-representative representatives of the total population does not mean that they had no political significance. The role of the advisers, who had been recruited mainly from the ranks of the intellectual dissident groups of the 1960s and 1970s, to the Solidarność movement in 1980/81 and the political significance of Neues Forum and the other opposition groups in the GDR in 1989 – again a mixture of 1960s reform-communist and 1980s Green-oriented minorities – shows how, in times of mass mobilisation, previously politically isolated and peripheral currents could be pushed to centre stage. Their isolation from the working class also explains, unfortunately, how they could be marginalised once again.

This all shows that what appeared to be highly ideological and politicised societies, such as the GDR, were in fact quite the opposite. Certainly during the antiquarian period they were characterised by

---

27. See Ehrhart Neubert, *Geschichte der Opposition in der DDR 1949–1989*, Berlin, 1998.

apathy, atomisation and demobilisation. Paradoxically, the short political century of extremes was therefore also the century of the end of politics.

If the PDS and the Left in general are to gain anything from the experience of 1989, the collapse of bureaucratic monumentalism and antiquarianism as forms of power ideology have to be taken as an opportunity to re-establish critical political ideology. For the social democratic and post-communist parties which emerged from the rubble of the Berlin Wall, however, the most difficult thing is to leave behind the monumentalism and antiquarianism and to embrace a new critical perspective capable of challenging the dominance of economic categories in the twenty-first century in the same way that the original Marxist approach did in the nineteenth. The key to understanding conjunctural developments, therefore, is an understanding of longer-term fluctuations in technological and economic developments.

Most commentators and analysts find the concept of the economic long wave and its determining influence on superstructural events unproblematic as long as it is an upward wave and the resulting socio-economic conditions and socio-cultural epiphenomena are relatively positive. Indeed, the term 'economic miracle' was coined to describe this phenomenon. Where the capitalist economy is concerned, however, they do not recognise that the long upward wave ended somewhere around the end of the 1960s and has flattened out and begun to turn downward since that point.

When things were going well, everything was attributed to economic success. Now that things are not going so well, everything is put down to individual weakness or wickedness or to the return of certain ideas for purely psychological or even genetically determined reasons of human nature. It would seem to be far more convincing, however, to adhere to the former explanatory model which apparently served so well and to recognise that the underlying economic and geo-strategic factors of the 1950s, 1960s, and early 1970s are now defunct and that the parameters of debate which determined the outcome of both the Godesberg programme and the Brezhnevite social contract are fundamentally changed.

Since the late 1960s and early 1970s, Germany and the rest of the Western world has found itself in a situation of general economic stagnation and downturn. The long upward wave of the first twenty-five years of the post-war period has turned into a long downward wave of falling growth and profit rates and rising unemployment.[28] At the same time as

28. See Ernest Mandel, *Late Capitalism*, London, 1975; Richard Day, 'The Theory of the Long Cycle: Kondratiev, Trotsky, Mandel', *New Left Review* no. 99, 1976, pp. 67–82; Andrew Tylecote, *The Long Wave in the World Economy: The Present Crisis in Historical Perspective*, London, 1992; Michael Husson, 'Riding the Long Wave', *historical materialism* no. 5, 1999, pp. 77–102.

unemployment was rising, however, social expenditure was falling drastically, leading to a decline in real incomes.[29] The inflationary spiral of the 1970s and 1980s has been defeated by neo-liberal economic policies but the consequence has been a drastic cut in the levels of productivity-based demand and an increase in the levels of state and private indebtedness.[30]

The Cold War in both its long and short forms is over. The West may appear to have won but the very factors which hastened the very welcome collapse of state Stalinism in 1989/90, namely economic and political bankruptcy, will not be escaped here either. The Left is therefore faced with a need to present alternatives to the prevailing neo-liberal orthodoxy in both East and West. It is my contention that this twin crisis, the real globalisation trend of the early twenty-first century, is behind the recent re-ideologisation of the political debate and a remobilisation of the working class as it is left increasingly exposed to the vagaries of market forces. The alternative to neo-liberal orthodoxy can no longer, however, be a simple return to the Keynesian certainty of social democratic governments of the past. Keynesian demand management has only ever been successful in periods of long upward waves in the capitalist economy. This is because the medium-term financial planning involved in Keynesianism has to be predicated upon the assumption of future growth rates which will enable the repayment of monies borrowed to finance short-term recovery programmes.

No economist today would claim to see any prospect of such growth rates. On the contrary, the five- to seven-year business cycles show a marked tendency for the boom periods to be shorter and shallower than the resulting slumps. Just as the private individual is unlikely to take out major credits or mortgages when faced with the prospect of unemployment, so governments are reluctant – indeed, are not permitted by the World Bank, the IMF and the Maastricht convergence criteria – to increase budget deficits in order to finance a recovery which cannot be paid for. The fundamental weakness of the tiger economies and the reason for their rapid decline are precisely because of their attempt to borrow and pump-prime their way out of a global crisis of overproduction, to artificially maintain levels of demand for their goods despite the

29. In Germany social expenditure grew at an annual rate of 4.8% between 1960 and 1975 but fell to 0.7% in the period 1980–1985. The overall figure for the G-7 nations was a fall from 7.6% to 2.6% These figures clearly show the weakening of the bargaining position of the working class from the mid 1970s on. Source: OECD, *Social Expenditure 1960–1985*, Paris, 1985, p. 28; OECD, *The Future of Social Protection*, Paris, 1988, p. 11, in Robert Brenner, 'The Economics of Global Turbulence', *New Left Review*, no. 229, 1998, p. 141.

30. Josef Joffe, for example, argues strongly that Gerhard Schröder's liberalising reform programme Agenda 2010 should be supported precisely because it recognises this shifted reality and that the unions and other social groups are being reactionary in opposing it. Josef Joffe, 'Revolte Rückwärts', *Die Zeit*, 24 April 2003, p. 1.

general downturn in their major export markets in the West and to ignore the structural weaknesses of an over-inflated financial sector.

The PDS today is being torn apart over precisely these issues. On the one hand, the Stalinist monumentalists and antiquarians around the Communist Platform and the Marxist Forum wish to stay loyal to a vision of the past which provided the security of a de-ideologised system of state rule. On the other hand the reformers around Gysi and Brie are attracted to a form of Left social democracy which is equally prelapsarian in its political vision. It is true that the critical approach of the latter group is trying to undermine the conservatism of the former. Yet the logical conclusions of their critical radicalism often lead them to adopt a third way position which is simply a celebration of West Germany's social democratic path, itself in turn an ideological defence structure for the adoption of Atlanticism.

The pivotal role of Gregor Gysi in the first ten years after 1989 demonstrates this very clearly. It is only now when the daily history of the GDR has been digested that there is a space for a leadership which can emerge from this relative anonymity, as it is the anonymity and security of life in the GDR which are, for many, a powerful pole of attraction. As Staud puts it, the new leadership were 'hard-working young members of the SED, dissatisfied with small areas of life in the GDR, but with good career prospects'.[31] This is precisely how many people remember the antiquarian years in the GDR

All of these factors – the national communist tradition of Eastern Europe, the democratic communist tradition within the SED, the international context of Stalinist rule and the relative social acceptance of the activities of the lower cadres of the SED – need to be taken into account when discussing the nature of the PDS today. The leadership is concerned to emphasise that there was a complete break with the Stalinist tradition of the SED in 1989. However, it is also necessary to emphasise that some of the traditions outlined above were relatively positive for, and continue to bring benefit to, the PDS. In recognising this, the main concern is not to throw the Marxist baby out with the Stalinist bathwater.

The Primacy of Economics

Now is the time for the economy.[32]

As Michel Husson points out, the turn-round in profitability started at the beginning of the 1980s as the free-market policies of the Right started to bear fruit out of deregulation, mass unemployment and a significant

31. Staud, 'Auf dem Weg zur CSU des Ostens', p. 6.
32. Uwe Jean Heuser, 'In den Zeiten der Wirtschaft. Die Neue Begeisterung für die Ökonomie', *Die Zeit* no. 44, 26 October 2000, p. 1.

increase in the rate of exploitation.[33] This trend took place in both the United States and Europe during this period although its impact in Germany was certainly less than that in the U.K. and it could be argued that Gerhard Schröder's Agenda 2010 programme is a belated attempt to catch up with the neo-liberal tide.

In the East too, however, the same structural economic crisis was wreaking havoc. As both Eric Hobsbawm and Frederic Jameson have pointed out, the Soviet Union was not able to 'delink' itself from this crisis.[34] Contrary to their contention, however, that there never was any chance of a complete delinking from the capitalist world. The East was forced to turn to the West for financial support – and therefore became dependent – precisely because its own form of social integration was even more costly than that of the West. The in-built inefficiencies of the bureaucratically planned Stalinist economies were masked only by the political imperative to maintain social cohesion, full employment and communal stability for as long as possible, i.e. until the late 1980s. And yet for the East too, the political century had come to an end in the mid 1970s. The political superstructure of both the West and the Soviet bureaucracy became fetters on the development of the productive forces.

Perestroika and glasnost were intended as methods of regenerating the Soviet economy, of taking the foot off the brake and yet it was too late. The inability of the Soviet bloc to do anything about the economic situation is the real reason behind the collapse of that system. The most important point to remember when assessing 1989 is that it was not simply a spontaneous and unforeseeable event which issued explosively from below in a desire for freedom, but an entirely logical consequence of a series of political decisions forced on the Soviet leadership by the economic exigencies of global restructuring.[35] The Brezhnev social contract and Honecker's 'unity of economic and social policy' of the 1970s represented the apotheosis of the politicisation of economics. In order for the state to maintain political control of society, it was necessary to prevent economic change. The resulting system of mass subsidisation and inherent inefficiency was both the only way in which the old system could survive in the short term and inevitably the one thing which would ensure its demise in the long term.

33. Husson, 'Riding the Long Wave', p. 84.
34. Jameson, 'Globalization and Political Strategy', p. 56.
35. 'Already signs of change are visible in the Soviet Bloc which could well have serious consequences for European politics in a period when western economies appear to be entering a period of economic downturn... The national question in Germany will in future become a much more important political issue and its solution will increasingly be seen as a way to solve some of the internal social and economic problems in both German states and the rest of Europe.' Peter Thompson, 'Socialism and the German Question', unpublished undergraduate dissertation, Portsmouth Polytechnic, 1987, pp. 50–51. See also Peter Gowan, *The Global Gamble*, London, 1999.

That the economics of inclusion and integration were determined primarily by politics is also clearly admitted by the leaders of business in the West. That they now see the opportunity to reverse the process of integration as a result of the demise of Stalinist socialism is also clear. Again as Gowan points out, quoting the then *Economist* editor and former Deputy Governor of the Bank of England, Rupert Pennant Rea: 'The penal taxation on which [social liberalism] was based was an import from Marxism forced upon the rich by the Cold War'.[36] Writing in *Die Zeit* recently, Christoph Dieckmann presented a chronology of events which were causing resentment in the ex-GDR. One of these elements was described thus:

> '1993: For reasons of "market correction" the Kassel Potash and Salt Mine company closes the profitable Thomas Münzer Mine in Bischofferrode. The six-month hunger strike has no effect. Thuringia's CDU Prime Minister talks of the "unacceptable face of capitalism". An unforgettable lesson on the primacy of the economy over politics.'[37]

And the former president of Germany, Roman Herzog, noted in a slightly less brutal way that:

> The systemic conflict of the twentieth century, unleashed by the Russian revolution in 1917, has come to an end. An antinomy under which we have all grown up and which split the world into two camps has been lifted. For the first time in history the idea of freedom has spread out and become almost unchallenged. And never before has there been such consensus that the free market is the economic system which best suits people's energy and temperament and which can therefore guarantee their prosperity.[38]

This represents the full and unashamed linking of the short twentieth century with the idea of the Russian revolution and sees 1989 as the return to a 'normality' in which the primacy of economics can be fully guaranteed. For these commentators, the whole of the twentieth century was a sort of European *Sonderweg* or special path in which too many people had too much say about too large a part of the economy. Indeed, the recent acceptance by the CDU of the Herzog proposals for further economic liberalisation has brought an end to the primacy of the social imperatives of post-1945 Christian Democracy in Germany and the considerable influence of consensus-oriented leaders such as Blüm, Geissler and even Helmut Kohl. Again, however, this not simply to do with abstract factional struggles within the political parties but represents the intrusion of changed external economic circumstances into the political parties. The primacy of economics requires the subordination of political parties to the world rather than vice versa.

---

36. Gowan, *The Global Gamble*, p. 259.
37. Christoph Dieckmann, 'Bitte nicht Aussteigen!', *Die Zeit* no. 40, 28 September 2000, p. 3.
38. Speech at the 41st German Historians' Congress on 17 September 1996 in Munich.

In a similar vein, Josef Joffe recently wrote in *Die Zeit* about 'the end of the ice age', drawing on Marx to show how the economic base was once again on the move and leading political developments:

> How do we notice that the plates are on the move again? Karl Marx, the man with the beard who had a better idea about tectonics than many a 20-year old in the city, would simply mutter 'the economic base'. Or to use the modern vernacular of a Bill Clinton: 'It's the economy, stupid!' ... Henning Schulte-Noelle of the Allianz group explains it thus: 'the demolition of the old system is evident. After the Second World War Germany had to be rebuilt and we needed a solid social system to achieve that. Now we are about to change that.'[39]

Or as Rolf-E. Breuer, spokesperson for the executive of the Deutsche Bank, puts it: 'The investor no longer has to accept the investment opportunities offered to him by governments, now it is governments who have to act according to the wishes of the investor.'[40] This statement would seem to reflect the apparently paradoxical assertion in the title of Breuer's article that free financial markets are said to be the best means of control over the activities of the state. At the same time, however, we are told that economics does not dominate politics. This would seem to challenge the contention that, in contradistinction to the situation under communism, the most important control over the activities of the state in the West is parliamentary democracy. Apparently, in the post-communist world, stockbrokers and finance capitalists will do a much better job. The Comintern has truly been superceded by the Capintern.

All of this represents the international, historical and socio-economic context in which we have to consider the position of the post-1989 Left. When we come to look at the PDS in the next chapter, we shall see that its literature and debates represent a mixture of nostalgias – monumentalist nostalgia for what never was – the German revolution of 1918/19, antiquarian nostalgia for what was – the GDR in all its aspects, and critical nostalgia for what might have been – a socialist Germany somewhere beyond both Stalinist and social democratic realities, – whilst at the same time projecting a serious alternative to a globalised and marketised future.

The question of Stalinism and de-Stalinisation remains relevant because the new Eastern European regimes remain essentially coalitions between the liberal factions of the old state apparatuses and the former dissident intellectuals. In almost all of the former Eastern Bloc states, the ruling bureaucracy has managed to transform itself into a ruling class with the simple administrative measures of voting themselves ownership of, rather than just bureaucratic control over, the means of production. Putin's role in Russia is a perfect example of this tendency, an old apparatchik who

39. Josef Joffe, 'Deutschland – das Ende der Eiszeit', *Die Zeit* no. 15, 2000, p. 3.
40. Rolf-E. Breuer, 'Die fünfte Gewalt. Herrscht die Wirtschaft über die Politik? Nein! Aber freie Finanzmärkte sind die wirkungsvollste Kontrollinstanz staatlichen Handels', *Die Zeit* no. 18, 2000, pp. 21–22.

uses the state only in order to further the primacy of the market. 'Classical' bourgeois parties, on the other hand, continue to play a relatively subordinate role. The GDR is, of course, an exception to this in that within weeks of its collapse it had taken on the party-political physiognomy of West Germany.

Even here, however, the dominant party, the CDU, existed before the collapse of the GDR and many of the leading East German figures in the CDU also exercised important functions under the old regime. In addition, the GDR was always an exception to the rule of analysis in Eastern Europe because of the nature of the unresolved German question and the fact that any fundamental change in the East was always likely to lead to the reunification of Germany. It should be noted here that a statement such as this, as obvious as it seems now, would not have been widely accepted on the Left in the mid 1980s when discussion of the German question was seen – with some exceptions in the Green and peace movements – as a nationalistic irrelevance.

From 1945 to 1956, however, the whole question of what Stalin wanted for Germany was essentially unclear and the uprising of 1953 took place within this context a few months after his death when the uncertainty was at its greatest. Stalin's uncertainty about Germany hung on until well after his death, however.[41] I tend to agree with those who argue that his primary concern was to rebuild the Soviet Union and that, when he thought that a unification of Germany in return for economic concessions from the West was in his interests, then that is what he pushed as his *Deutschlandpolitik*.[42] It was this uncertainty on the inter-systemic level and its effect on the SED which gave rise to the great factional struggles within the leadership precisely over the 'German road to socialism' and the role of the party in a united Germany.

This period of conflict did not really end until 1956 and Khrushchev's secret speech to the Twentieth Party Congress in Moscow. It was only after this that the Soviet Union was determined to consolidate the GDR and to stop any talk of possible unification. The period 1956–1958 was also the date of the last real ideologically based struggle within the leadership with the Schirdewan-Wollweber group in the Politburo and the

41. See Foschepoth *Adenauer und die Deutsche Frage*; Wolfgang Harich, *Keine Schwierigkeiten mit der Wahrheit*, Berlin, 1993; Siegfried Prokop, *Ein Streiter für Deutschland. Auseinandersetzungen mit Wofgang Harich*, Berlin, 1996; Leonhard, *Die Revolution entläßt ihre Kinder*.

42. See, for example, the debate on reparations and Stalin's tactics in Germany in the years before his death. Of the 101 billion DM (in 1953 prices) paid in reparations to the Soviet Union, 99 billion were taken from the SZO/GDR and only 2 billion from the West. See Arno Peters, 'Reparations-Ausgleichs-Plan', *Blätter für deutsche und internationale Politik*, no. 1, 1990. p. 12. Indeed, the uprising was partly a result of Stalin's policies of sucking the East dry. Those policies were only stopped after 1953. For a very clear discussion of these events' see Norbert Podewin, *Ulbrichts Weg an die Spitze der Macht. Stationen zwischen 1945 und 1954*, Berlin, 1998.

Janka-Harich group in the intelligentsia being removed from power and influence. After this period Ulbricht could rest assured that he was safe from attack both from Moscow and from within the party leadership.

Until at least 1958 and the marginalisation of the Schirdewan-Wollweber group, there were also some alliances between the oppositional milieu within the intelligentsia and the anti-Ulbricht currents in the party leadership. However, these alliances were never very strong because Schirdewan and Wollweber resisted to the very last the possibility of mobilising larger forces for their power struggle against Ulbricht and always hoped to be able to rely purely on Khrushchev's support in their endeavours. Wolfgang Harich, for example, always maintained that Schirdewan was part of the Ulbricht leadership and Schirdewan's own account of the 1956–1958 period of struggle in the leadership seems to confirm this impression. For all his criticism of the Ulbricht leadership, it is clear that he was not prepared to undertake anything which would damage the party in the eyes of the outside world.[43]

The same behaviour had also hindered the other oppositional leaders around Zaisser, Herrnstadt and Dahlem in using the workers' uprising in 1953 for their own reform purposes, leaving those such as Selbmann and Oelßner, who were prepared to challenge the leadership openly, exposed to Ulbricht's full revenge. The differences between Ulbricht and his critics in the Politburo and Central Committee were based not so much on matters of principle (the material which is now coming to light also confirms this view[44]) as on tactical considerations of a conjunctural nature. What is more, they usually reflected the factional struggles going on simultaneously in the Soviet leadership. The main themes of the opposition were those of the national question, the speed of the collectivisation of agriculture and, more generally, 'socialist reconstruction'. However, even if the Hungarian uprising had not forced Khrushchev to support 'the tried and trusted' Ulbricht against his competitors and even if those competitors had been more determined in their efforts, the question still remains as to whether Schirdewan really could have become a German Gomulka. The Ulbricht line of the fastest possible consolidation of the GDR against any new initiatives on German reunification emanating from Moscow was also in the interests of the vast majority of SED functionaries, who would have had nothing to gain from reunification.

The years 1945–1956 represented a period in which the policies of the bureaucracy came up against the resistance of the bourgeoisie and the 'old' political parties (including social democracy). This was therefore a highly ideological age, in which a politicised working class, which still had memories of organisational unity in the Weimar Republic and which had also in many cases either been in open or passive opposition to

43. Karl Schirdewan, *Aufstand gegen Ulbricht*, Berlin, 1994.
44. Ibid.

fascism, came back to the fore. Many studies show how the Ulbricht group on their return to Germany in April 1945 were given the immediate task of dismantling the spontaneous socialist movements and even soviets which had been set up by committees of social democrats and communists. The text of the KPD's founding declaration in 1945 shows this political priority quite clearly.[45] The party had to mobilise all its propagandistic efforts as well as the brute force of the SMAD in order to bring about this task but it did so on a clearly ideological basis.

The building of the Wall in 1961 was merely the necessary manifestation of the process of the division of the world into East and West and the establishment of a *modus operandi* between the two sides. Rather than being the high point of the Cold War, it should be seen as the precondition for a *détente* which was impossible to achieve on the basis of European instability and an open German border. Although this GDR interpretation was always rejected by the West for ideological reasons, it can now be admitted that it was as welcome to them as to the USSR and the GDR as it allowed a degree of normalisation of relations. Indeed, it could be argued that the real turning-point in East-West relations came in 1957 with the launch of the Sputnik satellite by the USSR. This showed that the Soviets now had a military capacity to carry not only satellites but also nuclear weapons into space and to land them where they wanted – such as in Washington – thus stabilising the Cold War into a balance of terror.

In this phase, the internal party opposition and Marxist-socialist currents in the working class and intelligentsia played a leading role in trying to redefine the nature of socialism in Germany and of trying to keep alive the chance of a reunited Germany. The removal of Ulbricht and his replacement with Honecker in 1971 were the main turning-point in GDR history in that it represented the final consolidation of the Brezhnev doctrine, as well as the Brezhnev social contract. It also brought the deepening of the social and political atomisation of the population and the end of monumentalist communist ideology as the main integrating focus of the party's activity.

By the mid 1960s the Soviet Union and the post-capitalist states of Eastern Europe had grown out of their post-revolutionary period. The completion of the internal process of transformation – which in the Soviet Union had taken a generation, in Eastern Europe on average only a

---

45. 'We are of the view that it would be wrong to impose the Soviet system on Germany as this system is not appropriate to current conditons in Germany. Rather, we are of the opinion that the decisive interests of the German people point in a different direction for Germany. We shall follow the path of the establishment of an anti-fascist, democratic regime, a parliamentary-democratic republic with all democratic rights and freedoms for the people. We also call for the completely unrestricted development of free trade and private entrepreneurialism on the basis of private property.' Leonhard, *Die Revolution entläßt ihre Kinder*, pp. 348–349.

decade or two – had reduced the bourgeoisie to insignificant remnants, so that the threat of directly counter-revolutionary and restorative tendencies either was purely an external one or would come from within the bureaucracy itself out of the inherent dynamic of its own disintegration. In the case of the GDR, of course, the open border between East and West had in some senses perhaps been of benefit for the state in that bourgeois oppositionists simply fled to the West.

By the same token, the threat of a direct military intervention by the West was as unrealistic as a direct bourgeois counter-revolution in those countries. The U.S.A. and NATO were, contrary to their own propaganda, always strategically dominant over the USSR but this dominance was only relative, which meant that a direct intervention would always have been an adventure with incalculable risk. It was the concentration on these two aspects of possible ways of overthrowing the Soviet Union which led many analysts to ignore the fact that the Eastern Bloc was crumbling from within under the weight of its own contradictions.

Compared with the Stalin and even Khrushchev eras, the Soviet Union was stable enough to survive right into the mid 1980s under the auspices of the Brezhnev social contract and the full and relatively successful industrialisation of a formerly predominantly rural economy. But the price which had to be paid for the creation of that stability led to its own demise. In a sense the bureaucracies of Eastern Europe became their own and increasingly willing gravediggers. When the end actually came, therefore, it was a result of the bureaucracies allowing it to happen, even promoting it themselves, rather than it being the result of spontaneous uprisings like those of 1953 in the GDR and 1956 in Hungary. The revolutions of 1989 were dissimilar to those of 1953 and 1956 in that the working class played very little part in them or came on to the scene very late in the day.

The East European states collapsed because Gorbachov made it clear that the Soviet Union would not intervene to prevent the increasing liberalisation of state and economy. This was a dynamic which the Gorbachov leadership believed they could control precisely because of the widely accepted apparent stability of the regime. They believed they could overcome the crisis of 1989/90 by making economic concessions through the increased marketisation of the economy, the shift away from mass industrial production towards a 'technical-scientific revolution' and an improvement in the standard of living for the masses. The recognition soon dawned, however, that in order to marketise the Eastern European economies it was necessary to open them to Western markets and investments and that the political result of that development would be that the people of those states would want political and social liberalisation to go hand in hand with the economic. The consequences of this for the GDR were obviously very different from those in the rest of Eastern

Europe but it is safe to say that the general context was one where neither bourgeois opposition nor the oppositional Marxist currents played a significant role. Now, a new generation of activists who were not part of the *Aufbau* tradition came to the fore in both the intelligentsia and the working class and they, in turn, came up against a 'modernised', de-ideologised and antiquarian bureaucracy.

In the case of the GDR, the importance of the international dimension cannot be stressed enough. There is no way in which the dynamics of development in a specific country in Eastern Europe can be understood simply in terms of either the internal contradictions within that country or the general contradictions of bureaucratic rule. The respective geopolitical situation of that country, the development of East-West relations, with their change from Cold War to *détente* and back again, and the growth of the Soviet Union's hegemony over Eastern Europe between 1953 and 1968 were of critical importance.

With the oil crisis of 1973/74 and the onset of mass unemployment and a balance-of-payments crisis, Western Europe saw a possible way out by increasing its exports to the East. At the same time, particularly for the Bundesrepublik, there was a switch to the increased use of nuclear power instead of coal, as well as increased imports of Soviet oil and other raw materials. The U.S. was seriously worried about this development and it is for this reason that Helmut Schmidt, as a social democratic leader, was concerned to prove bloc loyalty to the West by calling for a harder line towards the Soviet Union in terms of military-strategic policy.

For the GDR, therefore, this meant that the fear that both the West and the USSR had of the 'Finlandisation' of Germany – i.e. its neutralisation because of the growing economic interdependence between both halves of Europe – led to a contradictory dynamic. This contradiction lies essentially in the fact that the general economic crisis which faced the world in the 1970s was one based on a crisis of overproduction and stagflation in the West and underproduction in the East which could only be overcome by mutual exchange. The paradox was, that the policy of *Wandel durch Annäherung* (change through closer ties or coming together) had to be accompanied by an apparent intensification of *Abgrenzung* (distancing) on both sides of the Wall.

In the GDR there was a similar counter-productive paradox. Honecker's policies of *Abgrenzung* led to an increased feather-bedding of the social state, a guaranteed level of social provision and a technological 'catching up' in order to increase labour productivity. This proved to be the main Achilles' heel of the Soviet bloc in the entire post-war period. The bureaucratic reforms of that period were not primarily the result of pressure from below but were inherent in the contradictions of the Stalinist mode of production, which typically take the form of moves towards liberalisation: i.e. market economic mechanisms, increased freedom for intellectual activity and bureaucratically regulated pluralism.

Reform waves can clearly be discerned at this point which coincide with developments in the rhythms and forces of production, although this correlation is not mechanistically linked. In addition, there is also the tendency to move from the extensive production of heavy industrial goods to the intensive production of the third technological revolution. Although all of these factors were present in the GDR under Honecker, they were all compromised by geo-strategic considerations.

The reasons for this are clear. The move towards market economic mechanisms had as its corollary an acceptance of the possibility of unemployment. In addition, the use of competition between enterprises would undermine the one essential difference between the Federal Republic and the GDR which worked in favour of the GDR – namely, full and secure employment. The only claim to legitimacy which the SED had during the 1970s was the absence of unemployment and job insecurity at a time when mass unemployment was the major socio-economic characteristic of West German society. Although economic liberalisation in the rest of Eastern Europe tended to promote the reconstitution of an independent workers' movement as a result of the abandonment of the social contract, in the GDR this development was fundamentally hampered by the long break in the traditions of union organisation and socialist politics which Stalinism had engineered.

This is most clearly seen in the different roles played by the various working classes in Eastern Europe, from the central role of the independent workers' movement in Poland to the almost total absence of independent unions and parties of labour in the USSR, and indeed the GDR. The social weight of the working class and its practical ability to break the rule of the bureaucracy stood in great contrast to its political and ideological subordination and its tendency to articulate its demands in forms other than those of classic socialist democracy. This is closely related to the question of sociocultural physiognomy; and the Catholic nationalist attitudes of the Polish workers provide perhaps the best example of this. In the GDR the working class was hardly represented in any of the opposition movements and even the reconstituted SDP/SPD was led by church-based Protestant intellectuals rather than the organised working class. Even in the movement to emigrate from the GDR to the West, the working class was represented, though not proportionately to its social weight.

This development demonstrated very clearly the extent to which decades of monumentalist and, above all, antiquarian Stalinism in the GDR had effectively destroyed, atomised and finally de-ideologised independent working-class activity. At base this is the reason why the middle-class intellectual movement was the one calling for the maintenance and democratisation of a socialist GDR ('we are the people!') while the working class, once mobilised, moved very rapidly into clear opposition to any form of socialism ('we are one people!). For example – and even though it changed its position by December 1989 and by March 1990 had become a part of the Alliance for Germany coalition – the 'Founding document of Democratic Renewal (*Demokratischer Aufbruch*) states that: 'Democratic Renewal is a part of the political opposition in the GDR. Its members are opposed to the concept of reintroducing capitalist conditions into the GDR. They are in favour of the transformation of intolerable conditions in order to restore confidence in politics. We wish to see once again what socialism can really mean.'[46]

One example of the attempt to objectively categorise the nature of the transition of the regimes in Eastern Europe in the late 1980s is to be found in Dieter Segert.[47] He utilises critically Linz and Stepan's five typologies of Eastern European states,[48] but, even here, he concedes that it is difficult to arrive at a conclusion about why they collapsed.

> However, three paths to transformation are adduced: conscious decisions by the leadership; the collapse of authority; or pressure from below. But whether there are 'objective reasons' for choosing one or other of them which lie outside of the subject is not thematised. Thus, somehow, there comes a rejection of the ruling ideology and at some point or another relatively autonomous social, cultural and economic spaces emerge.[49]

The three elements named in this quotation would seem to me to exemplify all of the major reasons for the end of communism but they also need to be taken together. Most importantly, though, the order needs to be altered and the objective reasons which apparently lie outside the subject need to be reintegrated.

1. There was a definite and objective global crisis rooted in technological, industrial and economic change.
2. As a result, there was a definite erosion of the capacity to master change due to the hyper-politicised system of rule in the Eastern Bloc.
3. A definite decision was taken by the reformist leadership under Gorbachov to change policies accordingly (glasnost and perestroika).
4. Pressure from below forced that change in an uncontrollable direction once its scale and radical nature were recognised by the general population.
5. Hand in hand with these developments, an autonomous movement for change developed, which, however, was not necessarily in control of that change any more than were the reformist forces in the party.

These five points of transition demonstrate how it is simply impossible to separate out the objective from the subjective when trying to adduce

---

46. André Brie et al., *Zur Programmatik der Partei des Demokratischen Sozialismus. Ein Kommentar*, Berlin, 1997, p. 14.
47. Segert, 'Was war die DDR?'.
48. Totalitarian regime; totalitarian regime with sultanistic characteristics: post-totalitarian regime; authoritarian regime; democracy. ibid., p. 13.
49. Ibid., p. 20.

the reasons for social transformation. To do so is to hamper oneself unnecessarily in the name of dogmatic relativism. That relativism is as debilitating to intellectual processes as is dogmatic determinism.

The fundamental reason for the change after the mid 1970s is that surplus value could no longer be most efficiently gained through the integration and political participation of the mass working class. Apart from the sheer cost of the postwar Keynesian social settlement, technological innovation was beginning to undermine and challenge the productivist base of the Western economies. There were therefore two linked ways in which profitability could be restored. The first was through an increase in the general rate of exploitation by using the disciplining effect of the unemployment which economic crisis and technological progress were bringing about. The second was to force the pace of structural economic change and to take on the institutionalised force of labour rather than to soften the consequences of that change. In the words of Margaret Thatcher: 'there will be no more beer and sandwiches at No. 10'.[50]

The year 1974 is when this true *Wende* (revolution) begins. The defeat of the Conservative government of Edward Heath by the miners brought in a radical new neo-liberal leadership under Mrs Thatcher. It was to be another five years before she could introduce her new policies although the Callaghan government of 1974–1979 and its Chancellor Denis Healy were actually largely responsible for the monetarist policies imposed by the IMF and the World Bank. However, it would be as erroneous to credit Thatcher and Reagan with this as it would be to credit Stalin with Stalinism. These were trends forced upon governments by the exigencies of crisis. Perhaps the only difference between the Callaghan and Thatcher governments, for example, was that Thatcher could be proud of the policies which Callaghan had always had to apologise for. The same could be said for the shift from Schmidt to Kohl.

In 1974 it was Augusto Pinochet who was the first leader to introduce this new regime, at the point of a bayonet in Chile. His economic principles were those of the same school of deregulation and neo-liberalism which informed Thatcher, Reagan and the other marginally more democratic acolytes of the Friedman-Hayek school of monetarism. The year 1974 represents, therefore, the end of the ideal of the growth-based social democratic welfare state in the West.

For obvious political reasons, the same brutal attacks on the social position of the working class could not be undertaken in Eastern Europe. The objective strength of the working class in Eastern Europe actually meant that the regimes there were forced to take their own descriptions as workers' states at face value. That strength paradoxically prolonged the welfare dictatorship of the Brezhnev social contract in the East and as a result made the delayed collapse of the system that much more precipitate and radical. An

50. See for example Lord Campbell of Alloway, Hansard, 22 January 1997, column 742.

economy already hampered by inbuilt inefficiencies and backwardness was further undermined by placing authoritarian socio-political priorities above economic ones. The inflexibility and authoritarian nature of those regimes could not allow the workers to make any significant contribution to the running of the economy and they therefore had no commitment to its success or development. The major weakness was the undemocratic nature of the planned economy in Eastern Europe rather than the planned economy *per se*.

What this all demonstrates is the dialectical progression from political hegemony and back to economic hegemony. These are not separate periods based on some simplistic base and superstructure model but are intensely interwoven with each other. The primacy of economics of the first period is brought to an end by the successful rise to influence of the mass workers' movement. This takes place in both a reformist and a revolutionary fashion but the facticity of workers' influence, if not power, is real. This gives rise to the predominance of political considerations about how to keep the workers satisfied in both West and East. Economic decision making at the base is then fundamentally influenced by the exigencies of the socio-political superstructure. Eventually the costs of these political considerations become too much for the economy to afford and the integration of the working class into that social and political settlement becomes a brake on the further development of the rapidly changing productive forces.

What also underpins this development is the undeniable shift in the technological base of production itself. There is a wide and compendious literature on the end of the industrial working class and the shift from production to information, stretching from Gorz to Castells.[51] I do not intend to go into that particular issue in great detail here, other than to point out that the industrial working class has not gone away, but merely shifted geographically from its traditional heartlands in Europe and North America to the more historically peripheral areas of the world in Asia and South America. On a global scale, the industrial proletariat is actually larger now than it has ever been.[52] However, for my purposes in outlining the role of working-class parties in Germany in the twentieth century and the future of the PDS, this is a separate issue.

The reunification of Germany and the collapse of the Soviet Union represented the end of the politicisation of economics and the socialisation of foreign and military policy. In its place have come the economisation of politics and the imperialist instrumentalisation of foreign and military policy. Intervention, carried out in the name of human rights, is exercised selectively in order to spread Western values and protect Western interests. This is the global context in which my considerations of the PDS will be set.

51. André Gorz, *Farewell to the Working Class: an essay on Post-industrial Socialism*, London, 1982; Manuel Castells, *The Rise of the Network Society*, Cambridge, Mass. and Oxford, 1996.
52. Mike Davis, 'Planet of Slums. Urban Involution and the informal Proletariat' *New Left*

THE PDS: MARX'S BABY OR STALIN'S BATHWATER?

Now not only does life no longer rule and direct our knowledge of the past, but all the border markings too have been ripped up, and everything that used to exist has come crashing down.[1]

From the previous chapters we can now see that the revolution of 1989 was not one which affected just the GDR and Eastern Europe. Nor was it primarily located in a crisis of communism, but it was the expression of deep-seated global changes in technological development, economic dislocation and socio-political class relations. The whole of the world became revolutionised: the West gradually, the East in one cataclysmic event. The effects are essentially the same for both parts of the world. Nostalgia for the certainties of the postwar bipolar world, in which the years of stagnation were also the years of stability, exists in both East and West. It is this context which forms the backdrop for a proper consideration of the PDS today.

I shall also argue that the crisis which is at present affecting the PDS since its poor performance in the 2002 federal election and its virtual removal from the federal parliament is actually also a consequence of the very social and economic crisis which benefited it for so long. As Michael Brie put it in 2000, 'the same factors which led to a temporary increase in support [for the PDS] could also become the factors which lead to decline in support or even its eventual disappearance'.[2] Whether or not its decline is terminal or only relative has yet to be seen, and in answering this question the structural as well as the conjunctural reasons behind its recent drop in support need to be addressed.

1. Nietzsche, *Werke und Briefe*, p. 3898.
2. Michael Brie, 'Die PDS – Strategiebildung im Spannnungsfeld von gesellschaftlichen Konfliktlinien und politischer Identität', in Michael Brie and Rudolf Woderich, (eds), *Die PDS im Parteiensystem*, Berlin, 2000, p. 14.

In the West the current economic situation, in which social stability has declined in favour of market-driven labour flexibility, has generated the desire for ethnic and social stability. As a direct result of that, what might be called the 'Haiderisation' of the political agenda with right-wing populist appeals against foreigners, asylum-seekers and all other supposedly marginal groups, has taken place. And yet, at the same time as these right-wing forces call for social and communal stability and security, their programmes actually demand an intensified pursuit of deregulation, free capital markets and the free movement of labour. The xenophobic demands for exclusivity are accompanied by offers of green cards to anyone who can prove their economic worth, regardless of place of origin.[3] Ralf Dahrendorf came to the same conclusion when he stated in 2000 that: 'It is entirely possible that programmatically authoritarian movements will gain ground. After all Jörg Haider's FPÖ combines neo-liberal economic policy with inescapably authoritarian tendencies with regard to immigration, law and order.'[4]

In the East the situation is somewhat complicated by the fact that both the Right and the Left tend to compete for the same disaffected conservative and yet largely anti-capitalist and anti-liberal vote. The further east one goes in Eastern Europe, the closer the programmes of the communist or post-communist and nationalist parties become. In Russia, the Ukraine and Belarus, the consequences of shock therapy and mass immiseration have brought about a rise in the popularity of both openly Nazi and openly Stalinist movements, which sometimes even cooperate in the struggle against political and economic neo-liberalism. Although this cooperation does not take place in East Germany, the coincidence of the social values of their electors often does.

There are many studies which demonstrate that the social values of PDS voters in the East are markedly more conservative on questions of identity, community and order than those of left-wing voters in the West.[5] In this chapter I shall be investigating to what extent the PDS has to cater for those more authoritarian views or, indeed, whether those views are entirely negative. In the context of the previous chapters I shall therefore be looking not just at the uses and disadvantages of history but also of the authoritarian thinking which has grown out of that history for the PDS. One of the most significant efforts at a self-understanding of the party can be found in the book edited by Lothar Bisky *Die PDS – Herkunft und Selbstverständnis*, which issued from the conference held in November 1995 with the theme *Five years of the PDS in the Federal Republic: The Historical*

---

3. See Peter Thompson, 'Jörg Haider and the Paradoxical Crisis of Social Democracy in Europe Today', *Debatte*, vol. 8, No 1, 2000, pp. 9–22.
4. Dahrendorf, 'Die globale Klasse und die neue Ungleichheit'.
5. Deinert, *Institutionenvertrauen, Demokratiezufriedenheit und Extremwahl*; Neugebauer and Stöss, *Die PDS. Geschichte. Organisation. Mitgliederstruktur.*

Political Debate within the PDS.[6] In that book Helmut Seidel attempts to answer the question as to what the PDS is actually the 'successor' to. He comes to the conclusion that, if it is anything, it is the 'successor party to the workers' movement'.[7] That is the thesis which I shall test in this chapter

Monumentalism and Antiquarianism in the PDS

In August 1998, Lothar Bisky, Gregor Gysi and the other federal state leaders of the PDS wrote an open letter to Richard von Weizsäcker in defence of the democratic credentials of the PDS. It was designed to demonstrate to the public that the PDS was a party which was anchored in the provisions of the German Basic Law. The signatories of the appeal pointed out that, in the transition from the SED to the PDS, there had to be a period of consolidation and development of policies but that the PDS had the full intention of becoming a constitutionally loyal organisation: 'Along with the ideas behind Perestroika, it took the long repressed citizens' movements, the flight of thousands of young people from the GDR and the mass demonstrations of 1989 until we finally stood up and started to determine the fate of the party to which we belonged.'[8] The letter complained about the way in which the PDS was being presented as a completely unreformed Stalinist successor party to the SED: 'It has been completely forgotten today that the PDS emerged in 1989 out of a protest movement which existed among the members of the SED.'[9]

This memorandum to von Weizsäcker unleashed a storm of criticism within the party, which was only checked for fear of the appearance of division in the run-up to the federal elections on 27 September 1998. The success of the leadership's strategy and the gaining of 5.1% of the total vote and four direct mandates in Berlin, as well as a moderate and yet significant increase in the vote in West Germany, also helped to keep the debate under control. However, in the run-up to the January 1999 conference, questions of the interpretation of the party's past and its relationship to the SED and the GDR continued to play a central role in the discussions about the internal condition of the party and its long-term chances of success. The point being made in the memo to Richard

6. Bisky et al., *Die PDS*.
7. Helmut Seidel, 'Traditionen und Visionen. In welcher Nachfolge steht die PDS', Bisky et al., *Die PDS*, p. 20.
8. The signatories were Lothar Bisky, Gregor Gysi and the chairs of the State parties, Rosemarie Hein, Helmut Holter, Petra Pau, Peter Porsch, Wolfgang Thiel, Gabi Zimmer, 'Mit demokratischen Mitteln die politischen und sozialen Menschenrechte verteidigen. Brief an den ex-Bundespräsidenten Richard von Weizsäcker', Pressedienst PDS, no. 33, 14 August 1998, p. 2.
9. Ibid.

von Weizsäcker was that the SED had never been a monolithic organisation and that the PDS represented both a continuation of and a break with the traditions of the SED. The end of the apparent discipline of the cadre party and its democratic centralist organisational structure meant that the different non-organised factions and tendencies existing within it could come to the fore.

In an interview in 1998, Yvonne Kaufmann, at that time Deputy-Chair of the PDS, maintained that, although the PDS did not formally exist within the SED before 1989, many who formed the nucleus of the new movement were already in contact with one another and were motivated by the Gorbachev reforms to try and think of some new way of developing socialism.[10] However, she also conceded that there were just as many who subordinated themselves to party discipline and who were fully behind the leadership until the very last moment. Ironically it is the latter who tended to leave the party and those who were critical of the SED who stayed on to change it.

An important point she makes, nevertheless, is that politically the greatest challenge was to have created a 'successor' party out of the SED with all the problems of ideological ballast and material wealth which accrued from that. It would have been far easier for people such as Gysi, Brie, Bisky, Klein, etc., to have left the party along with the other 2.2 million members and to have gone to one of the other movements or parties to make a political career. Indeed it would have been easier to have created a totally new party. As Herbert Wolf points out, it was in the paradoxical position of being 'a new party without the formation of a new party'.[11]

The point, however, is that it is precisely because of that historical paradox that the PDS today contains all of the elements of socialist debate, just as the workers' and communist movement since the beginning of the century has contained them. There are the monumentalists and antiquarians in the form of the KPF and the MF, as well as the bulk of the membership of the party, and there are reformist and critical elements around the Zimmer as well as the Gysi-Bisky-Brie groups. These groupings are not entirely undifferentiated, however, and the election defeat of 2002 has led to a sharpening of the contradictions to the point of formal splits. Immediately after the election, Gysi, Brie and others around the reformist leadership spoke of creating a party somewhere between the SPD and the PDS involving themselves and possibly Oskar Lafontaine (what Eric Böhme called a UPDS). Subsequently the leadership of the SPD formally called on reformist-minded PDS modernisers to consider switching to the SPD. The Gera conference in October 2002, on the other hand, saw a strengthening of the Zimmer group and the consol-

10. Interview with Yvonne Kaufmann.
11. Herbert Wolf, *Woher kommt und wohin geht die PDS?*, Berlin, 1995, p. 5.

idation of the more eastern and oppositional forces within the party. Gabi Zimmer was reconfirmed as leader, against all expectations, and there was a clear reorientation towards creating a radical opposition to marketisation as well as a consolidation of the eastern perspective. This re-prioritisation – not concerned with the need to 'arrive in the Federal Republic' – is confirmed by Michael Brie's definition of the political climate in Germany since 1992: namely, the rise of the twin axes of social conflict between East and West and between social justice and the market.[12] Studies by Michael Chapra and Dietmar Wittich have quite clearly demonstrated how traditional socialist issues of social justice and wealth distribution increased significantly in importance during the 1990s. Between 1993 and 1996 a survey showed that the most important political issue had moved from the libertarian versus authoritarian axis (gender/generational/race) to that of social conflict (rich and poor/employers and employees). In the East the issue of rich and poor being important went from 58 per cent to 88 per cent. In the West the trend is even clearer, with an increase from 36 per cent to 80 per cent. The third most important issue became the social division between East and West (from 60 per cent to 79 per cent and from 50 per cent to 63 per cent, respectively). In other words the two axes of class and region became central, eclipsing what had been post-1968 West German political concerns.[13]

The collapse of the PDS vote in 2002 can therefore be attributed largely to the recognition on the part of the SPD that this dual axis had to be addressed. For that reason, the SPD moved leftward during the election campaign in social, economic and foreign policy areas and – with the apparent godsend of the floods in late August – was able to profile itself as a party which had the interests of the East (the area worst affected) at heart. There are two reasons why this might not prove a long-lasting strategy. Firstly, the actions of the second SPD-Green coalition government in the economic field quickly returned to market driven solutions and increased 'flexibilisation' of the economy. Secondly, of course, the floods receded. Both of those recessions did not lead directly to a full recovery of PDS support but there are some signs that the renewed disillusionment with the SPD could move people back towards the PDS in the East, if not in the West. However, as Michael Brie points out, the PDS is not yet in a position to capitalise on the structural problems facing the SPD-Green coalition from a left position. At the time of writing – in late 2003 – the fall in support for the SPD to less than 25 per cent in the

---

12. Brie, 'Die PDS – Strategiebildung im Spannnungsfeld von gesellschaftlichen Konfliktlinien und politischer Identität', p. 16.
13. Michael Chapra and Dietmar Wittich, *Projekt Gesellschaftskritische Potenziale. 1996–1998*, Halle and Berlin, 1998, quoted in Brie, 'Die PDS – Strategiebildung im Spannnungsfeld von gesellschaftlichen Konfliktlinien und politischer Identität', p. 24.

opinion polls does not seem to be feeding through into increased support for the PDS.

In order to mobilise politically around issues of social justice and the East-West axis, the post-2002 PDS chooses to emphasise both its eastern identity and its opposition to the market instead of the desire to become an all-German party committed to participation in government and therefore marketisation and flexibility. Michael Brie recognises this when he states that the PDS has to concentrate on becoming a left-wing East German *Volkspartei* (catch-all party) before it can move outwards and become a more radical and all-German socialist party. At the same time, he proposes that the PDS cannot mobilise all of the disaffected within its own ranks and should follow a policy of PDS Plus in which all centre-left and critical forces as well as the anti-globalisation and anti-imperialist movements would together form the basis for the relaunch of the PDS in a way similar to that in which the new social movements in 1970s West Germany led to the formation and eventual success of the Greens.[14] Whether there is an equivalent change of political culture in view as fundamental as that of the 1970s is questionable, but, as in all things, changing external conditions will change the basis of party support, and the very fact that both the SPD – with their Agenda 2010 reforms – and the CDU – with the Herzog proposals – have trimmed to the winds of neo-liberalism could create some political space for the PDS. Already there are the first stirrings of attempts to create a new party to the left of the SPD in the old West Germany with appeals being made to Lafontaine and/or Gysi to come in as possible leaders. At the moment this is only a very early sign of splits from the SPD in the West, but it does exemplify the way in which parties and their members respond to fundamental socio-economic change.

In an article in Debatte in 2002, Dieter Eissel comprehensively outlined the ever-increasing shift towards market dogmatism in the economic policies of the SPD-Green coalition. In the intervening two years, this trend has accelerated even further and with the adoption of the Agenda 2010, the SPD has now explicitly trimmed its sails to the prevailing neo-liberal winds. The adoption of this policy has, however, been pushed through against widespread opposition to its tenets from within the party itself. Unlike the situation for Tony Blair, who leads a largely supine party which was reformed well before he came to power, Gerhard Schröder has to take greater care when bringing in fundamental socio-economic change. He took power in 1998 still relying on the support of a party membership which had been sceptical of even the moderate Neue Mitte reform programme and with Oskar Lafontaine as an alternative leader. Schröder, by resigning as party chairman in February 2004, has had his Helmut Schmidt moment and is increasingly governing against a party which

14. Michael Brie 'Ist die PDS noch zu Retten?', *rls standpunkte* vol. 3, 2003.

fundamentally does not support him. Thus, even though Agenda 2010 represents a clear shift in economic policy towards the market, it is a relatively cautious step and merely continues an economic trend which started under Schmidt and which deepened under Kohl. Debates within the SPD essentially circle around the degree to which it is necessary to make a political virtue out of a market-driven necessity. The virulent ideological debate being conducted between the Netzwerker around Sigmar Gabriel from the West, who call for more freedom, and the traditionalists around Wolfgang Thierse from the East, who support more state, is the latest instalment in a conflict between the primacy of politics and the primacy of economics which has been running since the 1970s.

Recent polls of party members have shown that 60 per cent of members of the SPD consider Agenda 2010 to be 'anti-social' and 56 per cent have thought about leaving the party as a result. 32 per cent wish to see a return of Oskar Lafontaine to a leading position in the party and 58 per cent believe that Olaf Scholz, the SPD's General Secretary is dong a bad job. 72 per cent do not believe that the party can win the next election and its ratings in national opinion surveys languish in the low to mid 20 percentage points. 50 per cent of party members consider themselves to be left-wing and nearly two-thirds, 64 per cent, would rather go into opposition than give up their basic social democratic values. Even though the new agenda was pushed through at the extraordinary party congress in June 2003, only 49 per cent of members think it is reconcilable with those values. 73 per cent, on the other hand, are in favour of the reintroduction of inheritance tax as a way of raising money for the state.

On the other hand, it is also possible – as the more reform- and coalition-oriented members of the PDS argue – that the SPD and Greens are still more than capable of representing those critical of neo-liberal globalisation from within their own camp and that indeed, as they belong to precisely the same reformist and social camp as the PDS, then they should be supported in their attempts to implement a more socially neutral form of neo-liberal reformism.[15] The PDS is seen as a party which stands up for East German interests, which demands social justice and equality and supports the peace movement. In many ways these are traditional social democratic values in an East German setting. The real question is whether the PDS can come to be seen as a party which can realistically implement these interests and policies and whether it can mobilise a *soziopax* movement in the same way in which the Greens could emerge from and build on the *ökopax* movement. There is, however, a further complication in that the current PDS leadership is torn between participation in state government and the need – as Hermann Holter put it – to 'take to the streets'. That it should be Holter who made this statement shows the dilemma clearly in that he is also Minister of Labour in

---

15. Ibid., p 7.

the Mecklenburg-Vorpommern SPD-PDS coalition, thereby calling for a campaign on the streets against himself in power. The PDS's vote in the state election in Mecklenburg-Vorpommern, which took place on the same day as the federal election, fell by over 33 per cent and this drop was widely attributed to voter disillusionment with PDS behaviour in power as opposed to its promises in opposition.

This dual-track dilemma is, however, also compounded for the PDS by its need to integrate a historical analysis into its contemporary political programme. Opposition to the market, as well as continuing Eastern identification, automatically takes on a historical dimension, therefore, because the GDR in its antiquarian phase embodied both of those things to the exclusion of almost everything else. The Honecker years represented a form of GDR patriotism rooted in the absolute primacy of politics over economics. Yvonne Kaufmann emphasised the same point when she said that the PDS is a party which seeks both to look back to democratic traditions within the workers' movement and to utilise figures from the past, such as Liebknecht and Luxemburg. Yet at the same time it is a party trying to develop a programme which will look forward to the problems of a modern economy in a globalised context whilst not denying the role that many played within 'real existing socialism'.[16]

This emphasis on a forward-looking stance is significant. For the Stalinism debate within and about the PDS is not primarily about the past and culpability for the running of a Stalinist state but much more about political orientation for the future. Neugebauer and Stöss, however, make a fundamental mistake in maintaining that the retrospective view is its main problem: 'The magnitude of the ideological controversies taking place within the party is out of all proportion to their socio-political relevance. It is, as ever, backward-looking, neglects its profile as a modern socialist party and is therewith disengaging itself from the debate about general modernisation of the Federal Republic.'[17] The point is that the retrospectively imagined community of the GDR takes on different significance for different purposes. There is a large constituency which understands the term modernisation entirely negatively. To them it means the end of community, stability and comprehensibility in favour of flexibility, globalisation and economic liberalisation. This is what is also hinted at later when Neugebauer and Stöss state that '[the PDS] is a necessary and useful component of the political system in the Federal Republic'.[18] Although this highlights the role of the party as a representative of regional interests, it can equally be said that, without the retrospective element, there would be no party to play an integrative function. As a consequence those dissatisfied with unification may well go over to more dangerous forms of political expression. What is shown

16. Interview with Yvonne Kaufmann
17. Neugebauer and Stöss, Die PDS. Geschichte. Organisation. Mitgliederstruktur, 301–302.
18. Ibid., p. 303.

here is that history has both uses and disadvantages, which exist in a complicated relationship, and, as Jarausch points out, the debate about their significance is clearly defined by the political preferences of the participants.[19]

As an initial example of this complex relationship we can take Dieter Klein. Klein was one of the founders and main theoreticians of the reformist group Third Way in the late 1980s within the SED. He remains a reformist within the PDS and a member of its Federal Executive as well as a member of the Modern Socialism group at the Humboldt University in Berlin.[20] In that sense, he is well aware and critical of the history of Stalinism in the German workers' movement and its role in deforming the GDR. And yet he too takes a view of that history which is not entirely negative and is designed to rescue historical legitimation for the future of the PDS:

1. It is the party which best expresses East German interests and which has forced other parties to compete for the East German vote.
2. By dint of its historical roots in the workers' movement, its political programme and the interests of its voters, as well as its exclusion from all forms of power by the cartel of the established parties, it is the party which best represents the value of social justice.
3. Since the Berlin Programme of the SPD, in which democratic socialist values play only a very marginal role, the PDS is filling the vital role of a socialist party as they exist in many other European countries and which is essential in the mobilisation of countervailing power to existing social relations.[21]

What these three points demonstrate is that even someone determined to push the PDS in a more social democratic direction and who is broadly in favour of the removal of pro-SED elements from the party needs to emphasise the sense of continuity of a working-class tradition and to acknowledge the existence of the GDR as a social alternative to capitalism. Even someone like Dieter Klein from the critical tradition has to resort to elements of monumentalism and antiquarianism in order to make his point. The reason for this is to be found in the fact that what the traditional Left stood for, namely the social question, or the prioritisation of social justice over market freedom, is becoming central again after having been subordinated to the conflict between authoritarianism and libertarianism for so long.

19. Konrad Jarausch, 'Beyond Uniformity: The Challenge of Historicizing the GDR', in Konrad Jarausch (ed.), *Dictatorship as Experience. Towards a Socio-Cultural History of the GDR*, New York and Oxford, 1999, p. 127.
20. For an extensive analysis of the *Moderner Sozialismus* tendency see Sturm, '*Und der Zukunft zugewandt'?*, pp. 21–96.
21. Dieter Klein, 'Zwischen Ideologie und politischer Realität', in Barker, *The Party of Democratic Socialism in Germany*. P. 112.

The PDS's situation is part of a wider problematic. On the whole, attention is usually focused entirely on the date of 1989, *Die Wende* (turning-point/revolution), the point where history – depending on your point of view – either took a turn for better or for worse or indeed came to an abrupt end. The fifteen years since then in Germany have been preoccupied with a sense of disappointment. We are constantly tempted to conclude that this disappointment lies in the nature of the 'revolution' of 1989 and its consequences. The year 1989 is given a primary causative status, with symptomatic ripples emanating directly from it. One of those symptomatic ripples is the PDS. In the vast majority of studies, the success of the PDS is attributed to two separate factors. One is the existence of many hundreds of thousands of ex-bureaucrats and party members who simply wish for a return to the GDR. The second is resentment with the economic and social consequences of reunification. However, there is a further aspect to this problem. It is my view that the *Wende*, an event which informs so much of our thinking and research on contemporary German politics, culture and thought, is in fact of secondary importance and that the reasons for disillusionment with unification – and thus the PDS – lie further back than 1989/90.

The main reason for maintaining this is that German unification, as argued above, is itself merely a ripple, a symptom of a deeper and wider historical turning-point which can be located around the mid 1970s and which in turn is merely one of a series of related changes within the twentieth century. In consequence, the socio-economic situation in the ex-GDR is not primarily related to the mechanisms of transition since 1989 (in which the GDR has apparently been colonised by an unchanged West German society), but to the nature of economic transition which has embraced the world economy for a quarter of a century and which itself gave rise to unification.

The real problem facing Germany and its attempts to finally grow together lie in the fact that in 1989 East Germans demonstrated for unification with the auto-mythology rather than the changing reality of the Federal Republic. They imagined they would get the West Germany of the 1950s, but got that of the 1990s. They wished for the economic miracle but got the crisis of globalisation instead. Or, as Dieter Klein puts it, 'the irony of history is that just as East Germans rose up hopefully in order to participate in West German prosperity, the latter was just in the process of disappearing.'[22]

The disappointment with the 'present' has certainly strengthened the hand of those who seek a return to the certainties of the GDR. There are those within the PDS who do adhere to very strict authoritarian and Stalinist codes and who could be said to represent the continuity of a certain romantic nostalgia about the past. On the one hand, we find those who continue to see socialism simply as the nationalisation of the means of

22. Ibid., p. 117.

production and are, to a greater or lesser extent, critical of an 'obsession with democratic structures'.[23] They tend to be critical of the whole Stalinism debate and even, in the case of Sahra Wagenknecht, go as far as to say that the problem was that Honecker was not Stalinist enough, and that the end of the GDR was brought about by his policies of détente and making the Berlin Wall too permeable.[24] They look back with tenderness not so much to the Honecker but to the Ulbricht era.[25] These forces are to be found mainly in the KPF, the MF and at the base level of much of the membership, although these groups too are divided about the nature of Stalinism.[26] Yvonne Kaufmann maintains that they are a very small minority[27] but my impression is that the active members of these groups are supported by a much wider but unquantifiable milieu within the wider party membership. At the 4th Party Conference in 1995, for example, Sarah Wagenknecht received the votes of about one-third of the delegates when she stood for election to the Party Executive.[28] She was again re-elected to the Executive at the Gera Party Congress in October 2002.

On the other hand, there are those, mainly in the leadership, who emphasise the need for the PDS to become fully integrated into the Federal Republic. In August 1996, André Brie made his by now famous statement: 'we have to arrive in the Federal Republic once and for all. We have to develop a positive relationship to parliamentary democracy and the constitution,' thereby criticising those in the party who 'still stick to their old articles of faith'. For him the PDS had to become a normal party 'which is available as an alternative to the conservative government of the SPD and the Greens'.[29] Brie goes further in his criticism of the culturally conservative PDS and its adherence to old thinking. As the *Berliner Zeitung* reported:

> Somehow everyone was in agreement... 'Renewal', as it is called in the party, has to continue. Taken at face value, that would be the end of the matter. However, the Executive Committee showed itself yesterday in all its various shades and colours. The impetus for the debate came from the 'rebel' André Brie, who accused his party of not yet having 'arrived in the Federal Republic' and who wishes to make the party 'unbearable' for all the old post-Stalinists and who is demanding a promise to adhere to the constitution. Brie maintains that Stalinism is more widespread in the party than the size of the KPF would indicate, that the party is culturally conservative, that it is in danger of using its opposition to the prevailing system to wipe away any criticism or proper analysis of the GDR.[30]

23. Von Ditfurth, *Ostalgie oder linke Alternative*.
24. Ibid., p. 20. Sahra Wagenknecht is one of the leaders of the KPF.
25. See Schirdewan, *Aufstand gegen Ulbricht*.
26. Neugebauer and Stöss, *Die PDS. Geschichte. Organisation. Mitgliederstruktur*, p. 135.
27. Interview with Yvonne Kaufmann.
28. Sturm, *'Und der Zukunft zugewandt'?*, p. 18.
29. André Brie, 'Die PDS weiss nicht, wohin sie will', taz 16 August 1996.
30. Brigitte Fehrle, 'Mißverständnisse mit Brie. Der Parteivorstand ist nur scheinbar einer Meinung', *Berliner Zeitung* 27 August 1996, http://www.berlinonline.de/wissen/berliner _zeitung/archiv/1996/0827/politik/0031/.

Statements such as Brie's provoke in turn severe censure from the more orthodox members for being reformist and oriented exclusively towards power and office rather than opposition and change: 'At the centre of his politics is an increasing desire for power. Strategy is reduced to electoral tactics and the attainment of governmental power. Social strategy is reduced to politics which in turn no longer requires any social theory or ideology.'[31]

The reformists tend to equate socialism with radical democracy and do not overemphasise issues such as socialised relations of production, although they do talk of changing the system and are in favour of some nationalisation or at least an ill-defined sector of commonly owned property somewhere between the market and the state. For them, though, the question of ownership is not central. They are accused of having essentially moved towards a position of Western-oriented Left social democracy and of wanting to expel the KPF and even the MF but realise that a large part of the party's membership would not stand for it.[32] The leadership line on this issue is that to expel the Stalinists would be Stalinist. Bisky, for example, even though he is highly critical of the KPF and would like to see them leave the party, also declared: 'What are we to do? We are being pressured from all sides to expel the KPF but the idea horrifies me what with the history of the Left with all its purges and expulsions. Something like that would quickly damage the character of the party.'[33] Whether this statement is to be taken at face value is a different matter but it certainly also reflects the fact that any attempt to expel the KPF and the MF would also lead to serious disaffection amongst a large percentage of some of the most practically valuable members.

Michael Chrapa, however, maintains that there is not really a split between modernisers and traditionalists but rather between *kompeten-zorientierten Modernisieren* (modernisers who wish to take on responsibility and power) and *bewegungs-und werteorientierten Modernisier-ern* (modernisers based in the movement and in social values). The former are found in parliaments and leaderships, the latter at the grass roots, primarily concerned with social values and social security.[34]

31. Mitteilungen der Kommunistischen Plattform der PDS – October 2000, 'Wieviel Theorie braucht ein Programm?', speech given by Uwe-Jens Heuer at the Konferenz des Marxistischen Forums on 16 September 2000, http://www.pds-online.de/kpf-mitteilungen/0010/03.htm

32. This is certainly the position of André Brie and Dieter Klein, although less so of Gregor Gysi and Lothar Bisky.

33. '"Die Erneuerung wird aus dem Osten kommen", Thomas Falkner im Gespräch mit dem PDS-Bundesvorsitzenden Lothar Bisky (August 1994)', in Thomas Falkner and Dietmar Huber (eds), *Aufschwung PDS. Rote Socken zurück zur Macht?*, Munich, 1994, p. 313.

34. Brie 'Ist die PDS noch zu Retten?'

Clearly, then, different factions with different agendas are pulling the party in opposing directions. But at stake for all of them is the issue of the party's own roots in the GDR and the extent to which it can continue to draw succour from those roots. Michael Schumann shows how difficult it is for many in the PDS to actually break with the Stalinist version of the history of the GDR when he states that:

> The attempt at socialism in the GDR – despite all its failures, mistakes and even crimes – was a legitimate answer to a period in German history which had unleashed war and fascism and other unspeakable crimes in the first half of the twentieth century. It was a legitimate answer in the face of the catastrophic failure of the German bourgeois elite and the restoration of old relations of power in the Federal Republic. There is no need for an apology from the hundreds of thousands who took part in that alternative.[35]

The truth is however, that the very people who genuinely did want to create a real alternative to capitalism, fascism and even restoration were those who were purged, arrested, incarcerated, expelled and generally persecuted by those who took over the formation of the GDR. As I have shown above, the GDR was founded and created not only by genuine communists with the well-being of the German people and the future of socialism in mind, but predominantly by those functionaries of the bureaucracy whose only role was to implement the commands of the SMAD and the leadership of the CPSU. Equally, when Schumann maintains that 'the societies which emerged out of the October revolution have collapsed',[36] he makes a fundamental mistake because there was only one society which emanated from the October revolution: namely the Soviet Union.[37] The GDR did not issue from the October revolution but from the end of the anti-Hitler coalition and the requirements of Stalin's Soviet Union in the face of U.S. economic and strategic hegemony. All that having been said, however, the GDR continues to represent a system which at least attempted to prioritise the social and the political over the market. Thus, with growing historical distance between the reality of the dictatorial and artificial elements of the GDR, the attractiveness of the prioritisation of the social imperative also increases. Thus the *Heimat* the GDR represents for many, and the reason they vote for the PDS as a result, is a social one. The authoritarian nature of that system is then seen as a necessary corollary of social security. The same phenomenon can be found in nostalgia for Franco's Spain, Stalin's Russia and even Hitler's Germany. In times of insecurity, freedom is always less attractive than security. Opinion surveys show that the social question of the distribution of wealth between rich and poor also increased in importance in

35. Bisky et al., *Die PDS*, p. 22
36. Ibid., p. 28.
37. See list in Mayer, *Nur eine Partei nach Stalins Muster?*, p. 7.

West Germany in the 1990s, being a matter of great concern to 36 per cent of people in 1993, rising to 70-80 per cent by the end of that decade.[38]

What this means is that the PDS is not simply the successor party to the SED in the pejorative sense in which this is usually meant, but is also, as Helmut Seidel points out, one of the successor parties to the tradition of the German workers' movement of the twentieth century, which continues to prioritise the social over market freedom. The reason it is different from the other main parties is that it is still predominantly a political party, whereas all of the others – including to some extent the SPD – have become economic parties. As stated above, this does not mean that the other parties have decided to control the economy but that they have, to a greater or lesser degree, allowed market economic considerations to control them. A political party such as the PDS sees its role as that of attempting to control the economy in the name of social imperatives. At a time when the conservative governments of Bavaria and Saxony can put out statements which maintain that 'in the cities, poor areas may come into being in which reduced levels of health and life expectancy for some social groups as well as increased criminality are the obvious consequences of a low-wage policy.... However, that policy must be implemented in order to complete the shift towards an entrepreneurial society', it is easy to see why many are more scared of insecurity than authoritarianism.[39]

The search for social stability during a period of increased economic liberalisation will increasingly characterise political debate in the 21st century. The question to be addressed in this section is the extent to which the PDS is seen as an authoritarian party precisely because it resists this development. Are the authoritarian traditions associated with different forms of Stalinism holding it back or is the supposed conservative authoritarianism which the PDS represents merely a product of the defensive role which it plays for a significant section of the population of the ex-GDR? In other words, is *Ostalgie* ('Ostalgia') a call for the return to the authoritarianism of a Stalino-Prussian dictatorship or simply a desire for protection against the tides of globalisation? Dieter Klein touches on the same questions when he states that:

> the PDS is different from all of the other parties in that it sees the construction of a democratic countervailing power and the search for the institutionalisation of that countervailing power as essential to the radical social change it sees as necessary. At present we are seeing how society is increasingly being subordinated to the economy and how, more than ever in the post-war period, the drive for profitability at all costs is dominating the economy.[40]

---

38. Brie 'Ist die PDS noch zu Retten?'
39. Kommission für Zukunftsfragen der Freistaaten Bayern und Sachsen 1997, p. 23, in Brie 'Ist die PDS noch zu Retten?', p. 15.
40. Dieter Klein, 'Zwischen Ideologie und politischer Realität', in Barker, *The Party of Democratic Socialism in Germany*, p. 126.

Even this relatively modest social demand for the 'institutionalisation of countervailing power' would be seen as a call for the return to an authoritarian interference in the workings of society and economy. It is in this quotation, though, that Klein has identified the main problem the PDS will be facing in future. He implies here that the role that the PDS will have to take on is one of a Left opposition to globalisation and neo-liberalism on an all-German, if not an all-European, scale. This would, however, require an approach which opposes not only symptomatic aspects of the system but the system itself. He goes on to identify a very limited potential for practical opposition in the PDS, however, when he observes that the party is itself stuck in its East German ghetto and that its long-term role can only be to exercise some influence over a red-Green government: 'While it is possible that the function of the PDS as a representative of East German interests may decline as the other parties take over this role, there is a long-term logic which says that the role of a left-wing opposition to the SPD and the Greens will be of increasing importance.'[41] The question is, however, whether the defence of East German interests is something qualitatively different from exercising pressure on the SPD and the Greens. After all, what are East German interests and what are they being defended against? It is not simply a question of championing East German nostalgia against Western cultural dominance, but also of defending Eastern social solidarity against marketisation and social dislocation. In that sense, regional defence is synonymous with radical political opposition.[42] The failure to capitalise on this Left oppositional role can almost entirely be attributed to the fact that even in those areas in the East with the greatest possible objective basis for dissatisfaction with the neo-liberal agenda, there is a resignation about the ability of any party to stop the juggernaut. The SPD therefore reaps support as the party most likely to be able to at least stop some of the worst excesses of globalisation. Whether this will remain the case is open to question. It is at that point that the PDS's identification with the social imperatives of the GDR together with democratic renewal and socialist policy could come into play.

Ostalgie and disappointment with the revolution in the GDR are based on the fact that what people were ostensibly rejecting in Eastern Europe is different from that which the West felt they should be rejecting. The picture painted in the West that they were tearing down the Berlin Wall in order to get the market economy is only partially true and actually hides a fundamental difference between mentalities and attitudes in East and West. The reality is, that once the doctrine of the common European home had been pronounced, the people of Eastern Europe were willing to take the risk for real political change of superstructural elements of

41. Ibid.
42. Brie and Woderich, *Die PDS im Parteiensystem*, p. 21.

domination by the party in favour of a pluralist democracy (in the GDR at least initially socialist) and popular control of the political agenda.

That is, after all, what 'We are the people (*Wir sind das Volk*) meant. They were not primarily interested in a fundamental shake up of the post-capitalist patterns of capital ownership and the social provision which had arisen from the primacy of politics in the postwar period. However, what started out as a political revolution very soon tipped over into a social revolution with a predominantly economic dimension. Hence the refinement of the slogan into 'We are one people' (*Wir sind ein Volk*).

For reasons discussed in the previous section to do with the uniqueness of the GDR in an Eastern European context, this was always inevitable. It is for this reason that so many on the Left were – and remain – opposed to, or reluctant to accept, German unification. Winfried Wolf, for example, expresses a typically radical abstract rejection of German national identity found on the Western Left:

> This debate within the PDS is taking place in a Federal Republic in which a great majority of those who are resisting nationalist terror from the Right think of themselves as anti-national and internationalist and are appalled by a PDS which has discovered a German fatherland. And it gets worse. Almost all commentators speak of the 'PDS on route march to the right. PDS – on the way to Germany' was the title of an *FAZ* leader after the Cottbus Party Congress. *Die Zeit* sees the PDS as a new 'CSU of the East'. The *Berliner Zeitung* had the title 'PDS – die neue Deutschlandpartei'. This is certainly the way to get the PDS into the papers – but it is all negative advertising.[43]

The rhetoric of opposition to German unification – from Lafontaine to Grass – is very often coloured by predominantly moral and ethical questions which turn on whether the division of Germany is a just punishment for the crimes of the Nazis. At base, however, the fundamental objection is socio-economic. Even if not often explicitly put in these terms, recapitalisation and privatisation of the productive forces are seen as essentially counter-revolutionary and reactionary policies. As we have seen, those in the old guard of the PDS, such as Ellen Brombacher, explicitly see 1989 as a treacherous counter-revolution. As I have tried to show above, however, the objectivist vulgarisation of politics which characterises the Stalinist approach can itself only lead to negative consequences, in that the creation of objective conditions for something does not mean that subjective support will automatically follow.

Popular support for the PDS and the other post-communist parties in Eastern Europe fell away sharply after 1989 precisely because it was felt that the political changes which reunification and the end of Stalinism had brought could be achieved without economic cost. The drop in

---

43. 'PDS-Deutschtümelei. Kann es einen "linken Patriotismus" geben? Eine Antwort auf Klaus Höpcke', *Junge Welt*, 4 November 2000.

support for Left parties after the revolution in 1989, which led to an absolute majority for the Allianz für Deutschland in 1990 and the narrow victory for the CDU in 1994, demonstrates a phenomenon which was common to the major countries in Eastern Europe after the *Wende*. There was a short-lived phase of anti-communism, followed by a regeneration of post-communist socialist parties.[44] The reason for this is to be found neither in meaningless protest nor in a resurgence of some amorphous communist old boys' network, but in positive memories of the economic security and social solidarity the GDR provided.[45] These were the positive characteristics of the antiquarian societies in Eastern Europe which – after the negative memories of political oppression had begun to fade – dominated people's social consciousness.

It is therefore said that the PDS profits merely from people's resentment, protest and *Ostalgie*. If this is true then the real question should be what it is they resent and protest against and what they are nostalgic for. *Ostalgia* does not, I would contend, have anything to do with a return to the tyranny of SED rule. It is, instead much more likely to be about the desire to return to a period of social security and public provision, a return to the welfare, not the dictatorship, of the Honecker years. This is where accusations of social authoritarianism and lingering Stalinist thought structures are levelled at the PDS. In some cases, this is compounded by accusations of a right-wing dimension to the party's thinking.

For example, Gabrielle Zimmer (the former PDS leader) caused an outcry both within and outside the PDS by simply stating that she loves Germany. As a result, she was accused by many on the Left of pandering to *Deutschtümelei* (obsession with Germanness) and dragging the party to the right by claiming that:

> I – and here I represent of a whole layer of young people in the PDS leadership – had a completely positive attitude to the GDR. I saw it as my country. Now that it no longer exists I am sort of on the look out for a replacement.

What! Germany as an ersatz GDR?

> I don't want a new GDR, that's nonsense. I am looking for a new identity. One can be a Thuringian, a European, a citizen of the world, whatever. For me,

44. As Brie points out, in 1990 alone the PDS share of the vote fell from 16.4 per cent at the Volkskammerwahl, to 14 per cent at the Kommunalwahl, 11.6 per cent at the Landtagswahlen and 11.1 per cent in the Bundestagswahl in October before recovering to a point where the most recent opinion polls give it a constant level of support around 26–27 per cent: André Brie, *Die PDS im Ost und West – Fakten und Argumente statt Vermutungen*, Berlin, 2000; see also Dan Hough, *The Fall and Rise of the PDS*.

45. In a radio discussion in 2001, Vitaly Vitaliev criticised me for implying that they were in effect looking for the security of a prison cell. In one sense that is true but adjusting to life outside prison is a very difficult task and one which often leads some to reoffend in order to return to the security of the prison.

however, there is a national identity in addition to those things. It is easier for me to say that I love Germany than it is for Gysi or Bisky. They were born either just after or before the war. They experienced the Cold War of the 1950s and 1960s and they came up against the GDR in a quite different way from us younger ones. I think I speak for many young people in the PDS. We can come to terms with the conditions in the Federal Republic much more easily.[46]

This one quotation demonstrates quite remarkably the changes in attitude to the GDR, Marxism and the nation which took place within the space of two generations – a development which parallels the history of the German workers' movement. It shows that the older generation, growing up within the framework of ideological monumentalism, are still largely conditioned by those values, whereas the younger generation, socialised during the antiquarian period under Honecker, have a far more de-ideologised and non-political attitude towards their own history. For Zimmer the 'national' identity created in the GDR was something completely normal; the equivalent generation in the West still finds the concept of national identity very difficult. As a result, her ability to come to terms with being German is far greater than that even of many West Germans. For her, and this is also the basis for much *Ostalgie*, it is a question of seeking an identity in place rather than ideology.

Paradoxically, the collapse of Stalinism as an ideology has emptied the GDR of its political content and left a shell of memories of *Heimat*, order and stability. These are all concepts which the West German Left has spent many decades resisting in the name of socialist liberation. Paradoxically, Zimmer's generation of East Germans may well play a role in helping to normalise West German attitudes to their own nation.

The controversy which surrounds Zimmer's identification with Germany as a *Heimat* is predicated on whether one thinks this attitude is likely to play into the hands of the Right or, instead, to undermine their nationalist sentiments. One could argue against this that the existence of the PDS in the East of Germany has, to some extent and with the exception of some local success for the DVU, already prevented the rise of a hard-Right party. The growth of both the hard Right in the West and the PDS in the East points to the growing dissatisfaction with the apparent corruption of the old centre and to some of the problems facing European social democracy today as the neo-liberal aspects of globalisation bring the social question back on to the political agenda.

However, it is also necessary to ask to what extent the strength of the PDS is a cause or a symptom of the continuing de facto division of Germany. As Falkner and Huber point out, the PDS is so vehemently attacked by the representatives of all the other parties, although predominantly by Western politicians, that Eastern voters are forced into the

---

46. *taz* no. 6282, 28 October 2000, p. 3. For further contributions to this debate see
http://www.pds-online.de/partei/aktuell/0010/zimmer_taz.htm

arms of the party as a sort of counter-reaction.[47] This in turn helps to cement the sense of division, the feeling of being second-class citizens who, in the words of Wolfgang Schäuble, 'have not internalised democratic values',[48] so reinforcing the role of the PDS as the party which speaks for the citizens of the East.

Christian von Ditfurth, for example, asks the question: 'Who would ever have thought that *Heimat* would be the last refuge of Marxism-Leninism?'[49] And, although this rather faux-naive question ignores the fact that questions of *Heimat* and national identity have long played a role – if a neglected one – in the socialist movement,[50] it does touch upon one of the central issues of contemporary political debate, namely, that of the socio-ideological rather than merely the more commonly addressed political character of PDS support. This debate about the nation was also initiated around the time of the 1998 election when the leadership, and Lothar Bisky in particular, raised the question of national identity in Germany and what the relationship between the Left and the national question should be. As a result the PDS was attacked for being akin to the national Bolsheviks or the Strasserite Left Nazis.[51] The reason for this confusion lies in the fact that both socialism and orthodox conservatism tend to challenge neo-liberal and contemporary political orthodoxy and to put the interests of the collective above those of the individual.[52] Rolf Reisig emphasises this when he says that 'the new, predominantly neo-liberal line [of the SPD] does not represent the social democratic values which prevail in the East'.[53]

What has to be taken into account is that, for those who vote for both the PDS and the nationalist Right, programmatic and ideological factors are only, at best, of secondary importance. What these parties do have in common is the concerns and motivations of their voters, which are far more difficult to define than programmatic declarations. Several studies have shown that in the case of the PDS there is a great discrepancy

---

47. Falkner and Huber, *Aufschwung PDS*, p. 8
48. *Frankfurter Allgemeine Zeitung*, 28 June 1994; Falkner and Huber, *Aufschwung PDS*.
49. Von Ditfurth, *Ostalgie oder linke Alternative*, p. 63.
50. See Christoph Dieckmann, *Temperatursprung. Deutsche Verhältnisse*, Frankfurt, 1995.
51. See Johann M. Möller, *Die Welt*, 29 September 1998, p. 4, and also '"Die Duldung der rechstextremen Szene in der DDR ist zu verurteilen"', an interview with Lothar Bisky, *Der Tagesspiegel* 3 November 1998, p. 16.
52. The CDU has begun to realise the potential of this reality and has started to emphasise traditional right-wing political solutions, such as nationalism and the concept of the *Leitkultur* (this is the concept that German culture must be dominant). *Der Spiegel* points out that the CDU's candidate for Prime Minister of Brandenburg in the elections of 4 September 1999 tried to take some of the wind out of the DVU's sails by saying in *Junge Freiheit* (a right-wing weekly journal) that in the past there had been a fear of using the concept of the nation in the old Federal Republic and that this had led to 'certain distorted attitudes'. *Der Spiegel* no. 35, 30 August 1999, p. 27.
53. Ibid., p. 25.

between the political agenda put together by the leadership and the real attitudes of the bulk of the membership of the party. The membership retains a relatively old profile, with 58 per cent over 60 years old and 90 per cent ex-SED members, whereas the majority of its electoral support comes from young protest voters, civil servants and white-collar workers, with only some 15 per cent of workers voting for the party in 1994, rising to 17 per cent in 1998.[54]

The strength of the PDS and its continuing presence is shown by the way in which the SPD has had to change tack on relations with it. There are structural reasons for the PDS's continued existence and success and it is unlikely that they can be obviated by tactical ploys on the part of the other parties. Although the PDS has obviously established itself as a permanent and durable party in East Germany, there are still attempts to remove it as a competitor, especially on the part of the SPD. There are traditionally two tactics adopted to bring this about, ranging from a policy of seeing the PDS as the main enemy to one of hoping to demystify it. The first, propagated by those such as Stefan Hilsberg, is an aggressive one designed to help bring about the PDS's long-term destruction.[55] Hilsberg bases this call to arms on an analysis which posits the PDS as an unreformed and unreformable Stalinist party which is merely the continuation of the SED by other means. He is opposed to any form of toleration of or coalition with the PDS and maintains that it remains monolithic in its political character and not only represents the SED tradition in the ex-GDR but is also a direct descendant of the communist tradition dating back to 1918. On the one hand, this is an oversimplified analysis that ignores all caesuras in the traditions and history of the German workers' movement. On the other hand, it fails to recognise that an identification with the past is of benefit to the PDS. The more the PDS is attacked as Stalinist, undemocratic, unreformable and outside the bounds of acceptability the further its level of support rises. Since the election of 1998, when the PDS strengthened its position even further, this particular approach has lost much of its appeal, although it has not disappeared completely. The election results in Sachsen, Brandenburg and Thüringen in 1999 and Berlin in 2001,[56] respectively, would seem to indicate that an attempt to denigrate and marginalise the party via historical association is not working and that perhaps it might be time to ask whether those

54. Neugebauer and Stöss, *Die PDS. Geschichte. Organisation.* Mitgliederstruktur, p. 228 and André Brie, Die PDS im Ost und West, http://www.pds-online.de/partei /aktuell/0008/brie-studie.pdf. See this website for exhaustive statistics on, and significant analysis of, the electoral situation for the PDS in general.

55. Stephan Hilsberg, 'Strategien gegen die PDS', *Die Neue Gesellschaft/Frankfurter Hefte* vol. 43, no. 10, 1996, pp. 921–925.

56. In Saxony 22.2 per cent (up from 10.2 per cent in 1990), in Brandenburg 23.3 per cent (up from 13.4 per cent in 1990), in Thüringen 21.4 per cent (up from 9.7 per cent in 1990). Forschungsgruppe Wahlen at http://www.politik-digital.de

historical associations are not the very things helping to strengthen its position in Germany today.

Richard Schröder, on the other hand takes a more conciliatory line towards the PDS, presenting it as an undefined party and arguing that its many different wings are so far apart that it is in fact several parties in one.[57] Schröder maintains that the members of the old SED can be divided into three groups. The first were the careerists who were also the first to leave the party in 1989 (and who either left political activity altogether or actually joined one of the bourgeois parties rather than the SPD). The second were those who wanted to use the SED in order to influence and change the GDR. The third were those who saw socialism in its GDR form as the apotheosis of human achievement to date.

He also maintains that the PDS is formed largely out of a mixture of the second and third groups and that, although coalitions with it should be avoided, the issues which it raises and the support it garners have to be taken seriously. The party itself has to be challenged in a 'friendly' way, hoping that, in doing so, the PDS will 'social-democratise' itself and the communist wing will split off. Recent developments have shown this tactic to be much more realistic. The communist wing has not split off but is certainly being constantly eclipsed and increasingly plays a mascot role. On the other hand there has been a clearly identifiable trend towards the social-democratisation of the party. *The Ingolstadt Manifesto* of 1993, for example, represented an attempt by the leadership, and in particular Gysi, to create a more conciliatory approach to the Federal Republic and its social market economy.[58]

There are, however, problems with this strategy too. Firstly, the PDS is unlikely to fully social-democratise itself as long as it can retain such high levels of support by remaining an East German regional party with an oppositional socialist profile. An essential part of this profile is indeed a refusal to write off the communist tradition and the experience of the GDR. Without an identification with Eastern interests, the PDS has no reason to exist, just as the GDR found it had no reason to exist after 1989.

Secondly, there is no guarantee that PDS voters would simply shift *en masse* to the SPD. It is perhaps more likely that, given the values which many of the older voters and a majority of the members of the PDS have, a hard-Right alternative could emerge in the form of a reinvigorated but now Eastern German Republikaner/DVU or other German nationalist party. The Right has recognised this East German potential as well and campaigns there with slogans which are as anti-capitalist as they are xenophobic.[59] It is this recognition, which lay behind the new isolation-

57. Richard Schröder, 'SED, PDS und die Republik', *Die Neue Gesellschaft/Frankfurter Hefte* vol. 43, No. 10, 1996, pp. 912–921.
58. Sturm, '*Und der Zukunft zugewandt'?*, pp. 196–210.
59. See, for example, the NPD Partei Programm at http://home.t-online.de/home/National/programm.htm

ist approach of the late 1990s and the concomitant emphasis on German national identity.

The question for the PDS is whether it is possible to defend the idea of community and 'communism' in a Germany dominated by the compounded ideologies of abstract anti-nationalism and an increasingly neo-liberal economic outlook, without appearing socially authoritarian. Or is it necessary to accept the accusation in order to be able to pursue socialist policies at all? If so, what sort of problems does this cause for the PDS in its relationships with a predominantly libertarian Western Left and an increasingly neo-liberal SPD? The PDS is increasingly described as a nationalist and socialist party, if not yet a National Socialist one. As Stefan Berg has pointed out, there now exists in the ex-GDR the *Menschengemeinschaft* (community of people) which Ulbricht once dreamed of.[60] Whether it is a socialist one is another question. The PDS tends to represent those who have a memory (false or not) of social cohesion or those who feel that one should be regained against the tide of individualism sweeping in from the West. Too often, though, this desire for a *Menschengemeinschaft* is misidentified as a desire for *Volksgemeinschaft* (community of the People – the Nazi term for German society).[61]

A regionalist sense of community is a phenomenon which can have a very durable and tenacious existence and it is something which is often strengthened by a sense of resentment and inferiority towards the metropolitan centre. The U.K., Spain, France and Italy all have these regional conflicts. Something which Germany may have to come to terms with over the coming years is the fact that it too will become a multinational as well as a multicultural state. As Peter Welker asks, have the East Germans become the 'largest national minority in Germany'?[62]

One can usefully compare East Germany to that of the position of Scotland within the U.K. The Act of Union in 1707 could be seen in some senses as a close parallel to German unification in 1990. Of course, in this case there was not the unification of two disparate economic modes of production, but there was the perceived annexation of a piece of territory which, though economically and politically advantageous to the capitalist development of the U.K., certainly also created a sense of resentment on the part of the smaller nation towards the larger which still persists. The people of the ex-GDR view West Germany very much in the same way as the people of Scotland see the English. They know they are tied together by linguistic, historical, economic, social and familial links and yet they

60. Stefan Berg, *Das lange Leben der DDR*, Berlin, 1995, p. 15.
61. For a good example of this suspicion on the Left towards the concept of the nation, see the analysis and collection of documents in *Die Linke und die 'soziale Frage'. Wie rechte Wahlerfolge, Nationalismus und Rassismus zusammenhängen*, http://www.nadir.org/nadir/periodika/bahamas/auswahl/web40.htm
62. Peter Welker (ed.), *Die Sache mit der Nation 1. Nachdenken über ein für Linke schwieriges Thema. Materialien zweier Fachtagungen 9.Mai 1993, 27 November 1993*, Berlin, 1994, p. 10.

feel themselves to be entirely separate in one specific way, namely, the way they feel they have been bought up and used by the English ruling class. There is also a very clear class element in the Scottish/English split. The PDS plays the same role in Germany that the post-1984 SNP or, indeed, the new Scottish Socialist Party, does in Scotland. The former is a nationalist party with left-wing elements, the latter, a left-wing party with nationalist elements. They represent the interests of a specific region/nation and yet they are not xenophobic in their outlook other than towards the metropolitan centre.[63] Nearly 300 years after the Act of Union the outcome of a referendum on the issue of Scottish devolution showed how deep-seated this resentment can be, despite the fact that the objective economic trend in state formation is towards internationalisation and the end of the nation state rather than its reconstitution.

Indeed, the very fact that the world is becoming increasingly globalised in economic terms leads to the reinvigoration of notions of community and nation. The centrifugal forces of modern production, which tear at what were stable and reliable social structures and replace them with concepts of autonomy, liberalisation and flexibility, seem to create a backlash of nostalgia for social stability which, in the case of the GDR, was almost universally perceived as stifling but also secure.

Paradoxically, therefore, it could be argued – as does Friedrich Jaeger – that the nostalgia for the GDR is more similar to the American theoretical tradition of the civil society – a tradition 'which as the sum of social communities creates and constantly renews the elements of its own cultural integration on which it then thrives as a society,'[64] than it is to the ideal of the West German bourgeois society. As Jaeger goes on to point out, within the concept of civil society economic rationale and cultural identity are seen as indivisible, whereas in the concept of the 'bourgeois society' they are often treated as separate entities. In the case of German unification, the attempt to impose a 'bourgeois' form of West German identity on to a social tradition rooted more in notions of civil community is bound to cause friction and fundamental misunderstanding.

This conclusion would seem, however, to imply that the PDS, in its attempt to maintain the concept and form of civil community attained in the ex-GDR, has essentially adopted a communitarian position not that far removed from that of the Clinton/Blair project. Indeed, the Blair project in Britain is heavily influenced by the communitarian ideas of

---

63. In fact, it is perhaps more similar to the new Scottish Socialist Party, which emerged largely out of the Trotskyist movement and which is now a radical left-wing party with nationalist elements and scored remarkable success at the last Scottish parliamentary elections, gaining four seats.

64. Friedrich Jaeger, 'Gesellschaft und Gemeinschaft. Die Gesellschaftstheorie des Kommunitarismus und die politische Ideengeschichte der "civil society" in den U.S.A.', in Thomas Mergel and Thomas Welskopp (eds), *Geschichte Zwischen Kultur und Gesellschaft. Beiträge zur Theoriedebatte*. Munich, 1997, p. 306.

Etzioni and insists on social cohesion and personal responsibility, concepts which are often seen as socially authoritarian. It uses the language of authority in order to try to hold together communities which are flying apart in the process of modernisation. Equally, the PDS seems to tap into very similar sorts of concerns. Its very strength is in its identification with a group of people who feel themselves to be under threat from all manner of external forces which, before 1989, had very little ingress into their stable communities. Thus the PDS's mobilisation of *Ostalgie* is seen as characteristic of a party which cannot break away from the old political structures associated with the GDR and is therefore judged to be 'authoritarian'.

However, the PDS's social activities can be seen to be qualitatively different from the communitarian values expounded by Clinton and Blair. The difference lies in one of the strong points of the PDS, in that its basic ideology contains a strong anti-capitalist element. It locates the sense of alienation, which East Germans undoubtedly feel, firmly within the socio-economic consequences of free-market capitalism, rather than in some amorphous sense of lost identity. If it is true that others are coming in and taking away East German jobs and if it is true that criminality is rising and that communities are disintegrating then the question is why this is happening. Where the blame is put for these phenomena is fundamentally different in the PDS compared with New Labour or the New Democrats.

The Blair leadership tends to ascribe social disintegration to a form of moral decline linked to the end of religion and abstract notions of social cohesion existing in some ahistorical and non-ideological vacuum. Thus, in classic bourgeois terms, as Jaeger describes them, they see no contradiction in propagating the deepening and widening of the Thatcherite project of total labour flexibility and free markets alongside the call for the re-establishment of notions of community and social responsibility. The PDS, on the other hand, still adheres to a materialist analysis of these social epiphenomena. Social decline is firmly linked to economic factors, unemployment is seen as a basic component of free-market economic strategy and the resulting social consequences are seen as fundamentally determined by the nature of late-capitalist modes of production. It is for this reason that the SPD's recent attempts to find an ideological base in notions of the 'civil bourgeois society' will be less than convincing as long as the centrifugal tendencies inherent in 'modernisation' are given priority.

It is true that the Gysi, Bisky, Brie leadership would like to move away from this analysis towards a more Blairite turn of phrase and analysis, but it is the very presence of those elements most disliked by the dominant Western view of the PDS which prevents this. Again, therefore, this essentially progressive analysis of the consequences of German reunification is presented merely as a reactionary desire for the re-establishment of the GDR, whereas in reality it represents an attempt to plot a survival course through the negative social reality of global capitalism.

The sense of social isolation and confusion which is now undoubtedly present in the ex-GDR is therefore clearly represented in opinion-poll and survey data conducted in the ex-GDR. The most exhaustive surveys conducted to date are analysed in Neugebauer and Stöss, where the traditional Left/Right axis for determining social values is replaced with intersecting authoritarian/liberal social justice/free market axes. With this repositioning and reinterpretation of social values, we find in many cases that PDS voters and members are revealed as being authoritarian and heavily oriented towards social justice rather than the free market. With this presentation of data, it is also apparently easy to show that, in terms of social values, PDS voters can hardly be distinguished from those of the hard-Right Republikaner.[65] Again however, this sort of interpretation of raw data fundamentally distorts the thinking and motivation behind the apparent overlap of superficial responses to public-opinion surveys. The social psychology of the average East German is not determined by some Prussian-fascist authoritarian personality trait but by their experience of unification, conflated with their ever-fading memories of the reality of the GDR.

It is this almost complete misunderstanding of the East by the West which helps to cement and exacerbate the division between the two parts of Germany. The reason for this, I believe, lies also in the specific history of the old Federal Republic, which was, as Brandt famously said, an 'economic giant but a political dwarf'.[66] West German identity in the entire postwar period was also focused almost entirely on economic factors and material incentives rather than political engagement. And yet the economic prosperity they gained was predicated on the same politicisation of socio-economic priorities as was the case in the GDR. For West Germans to admit that the basis of their state and their history was not so very different from that of the GDR is a complicated psychological act. In a sort of mirror image of West Germany, East German identification with the GDR is with its socio-economic structures, with its collectivist and non-market-oriented values and not with the political dictatorship of the party elite. If the West Germans had the economic miracle and deutschmark patriotism as an ersatz identity, then the East Germans had their antiquarian Niche Society. What both had in common was a propensity not to examine the underlying geo-strategic and historical conditions for their social and economic systems. The continuing success of the PDS is therefore predicated not on some rejection of the forms of socio-economic organisation in the GDR but on its continued

65. See Neugebauer and Stöss, *Die PDS. Geschichte. Organisation. Mitgliederstruktur*, p 290.
66. http://www.gegenstandpunkt.com/msz/html/87/87_5/brandt.htm.

exposition of a socio-economic alternative to the capitalist market and a propagation of the priority of social cohesion.

For the time being, this continues to be the strategy followed by the party as a whole. Its continued success is therefore not just a geographical phenomenon but also an ideological one located in its ability to present itself as fundamentally different from the SPD and the Greens. Of course, the political consequences of this are obvious. Anyone who stands against the freedom of the market is deemed to be against freedom *per se*. The logic used is that the PDS must be socially and politically authoritarian, if not Stalinist, because it continues to adhere at least partially to an economic analysis which does not fit in with the needs of capital and has not made the sort of Godesbergian conversion which was once required of the SPD.

The problem for the PDS with such a conversion would be that it would then simply be a smaller version of the SPD and would quickly cease to have any real function. At present its only role is as a party to the left of the SPD, anchored in its geographical homeland and social milieu. Even André Brie, the most vocal of those wishing for a social-democratisation of the PDS and a more serious orientation towards the West, recognises the limitations facing the party. On the one hand, he calls quite clearly for an orientation towards *Realpolitik*: 'The new responsibility of the PDS rests in the fact that its voters no longer simply see it as a representative of eastern interests and left-wing homilies and legitimate protest but are expecting it to get involved in representing their interests politically and effectively. If it does not meet these expectations its existence will once again be endangered.'[67] On the other hand, he recognises that these demands are unrealistic for the foreseeable future:

> The path to acceptance in West Germany will be long and hard. A structural East-West asymmetry will prevail for the foreseeable future. The ever-present self-delusion of local party executives in the West only serves to sharpen their voluntaristic and illusionary nature as well as the constant and unavoidable (and equally ignored) problems which emerge as a consequence. Alongside the internal party differences, the PDS will continue to be confronted by the problem of not being sufficiently anchored in West German society, not being able to take up impulses from it or to be involved in its existing social movements.[68]

In this second quotation, Brie is trying to transfer the blame for the lack of success in West Germany on the nature of the PDS members there and yet, as he also points out, perhaps the greatest problem is that the SPD – his preferred coalition partner – is shifting to the Right so rapidly that the PDS cannot do business with it without losing its own political *raison d'être*. Although Gabrielle Zimmer was the leadership's chosen candidate as Bisky's and Gysi's successor, it is hard to see how her turn to the East

67. Brie, *Die PDS im Ost und West – Fakten und Argumente statt Vermutungen*, p. 6.
68. Ibid., p. 5.

was ever supposed to achieve the break-out out from the ghetto: something which Brie has clearly always wanted to achieve.[69] The shift back to the modernisers around Bisky in 2003 is a risky and – in all probability – temporary measure, which has done nothing to reduce the level of internal division between parliamentarist reformism and oppositionist radicalism.

Another reason for the perception of the PDS as an authoritarian party is more to do with the political heritage of those doing the analysis than the subjects of that analysis. In this case, the typical Western post-1968 anti-authoritarian perspective is applied to a society which had no 1968 and which is not obsessed with retrospective anti-Nazism and abstract anti-nationalism in the same way as its Western counterpart. The view, therefore, that the PDS is close to right-wing values is based on a criticism of its adherence in Eastern Germany to what are seen as values traditionally associated with the Right in Western Germany. But again, what are seen as negative values in a capitalist society – discipline, law and order, thrift and an identification with *Heimat*[70] – are not necessarily negative when felt by those socialised in a society which considered itself a socialist community of the people (*sozialistische Menschengemeinschaft*) with a high degree of collective identification and social cohesion.

Of course, it can be argued that values such as these, in themselves and regardless of their socio-historical context, tend towards exclusivist or xenophobic attitudes. The rise of neo-Nazi movements and attacks on foreigners are often pointed to as prime examples of this.[71] And yet every study shows that those engaged in such activities were not of the generation which is traditionally associated with the above values. Rather, such attacks are carried out by the young disaffected generation socialised in the closing years of the GDR and during the years since the fall of the Berlin Wall. In addition the high point of right-wing political activity and racist violence is now passed, even though they remain present. Those of the older GDR-nostalgic generation may well be conservative in their outlook but one has to ask what it is they wish to conserve and whether or not they have a point in doing so. That they vote PDS should be held neither against them nor against the PDS.

The ability of the PDS to integrate and channel such potentially xenophobic sentiment into a socio-political understanding of the underlying crisis is infinitely preferable to its mobilisation by the forces of the Right. For example, the PDS is in the forefront of anti-racist campaigns to extend active and passive voting rights to non-German citizens, supported the abolition of the *Jus Sanguinis* German citizenship laws, and was, with the

---

69. See my interview with André Brie, 'A purely East German alternative is an illusion', *Debatte*, vol. 2, no. 2, 1994, pp. 16–26
70. 'Schnell ans Meer', *Der Spiegel*, no. 47, 1995, p. 50.
71. *Die Linke und die 'soziale Frage'*, http://www.nadir.org/nadir/periodika/bahamas/auswahl/web40.htm

Greens, one of the only real opponents of the changes to the asylum laws which were carried through by the CDU/FDP coalition with SPD support in the face of a panic about the rise of the hard Right and attacks on foreigners. At the same time, however, it can offer a sense of *Heimat* to its voters, something which no other party in Germany, apart from the CSU, can do.

If we compare the PDS's attempts to channel the right-wing potential with the SPD's disastrous attempt to utilise it in the Hamburg state elections in September 1997, the outcome is clear to see. In the ex-GDR, the hard Right gained relatively little electoral support. In Hamburg in 1997 the Republikaner and the DVU between them took 7 per cent of the vote. In the current deflationary downward spiral and a period of modernisation of the economic base, there is indeed competition for jobs and that competition plays itself out between different groups of workers and their wage levels. In the free market, one of the only ways to compete is to drive wages down to a level where they undercut other countries' workers. Cheap labour undercutting high-cost labour in the advanced industrial countries, or what used to be the metropolitan centres of empire on which the traditional social-democratic, Fordist and productivist vote was based, is bound to cause social tension. It is simply a question of who gets the blame for this, the economic system or its victims. That the PDS blames the system rather than the victims and does not join in the prevailing mood of xenophobia should be entirely welcome.

In conclusion, we can say that the PDS has certain trends and tendencies as well as supporters and voting groups which can be seen as relatively authoritarian. In the words of Neugebauer and Stöss, however, all this shows is that the PDS is a 'completely normal party'.[72] Where it is different to the other parties, including the Greens, is in its continuing commitment to a radical analysis of social phenomena and a totalising theory based at least partially on Marxist historical materialism. The problem for the PDS is that, in these days of neo-liberal individualism, all totalising theories are automatically seen as authoritarian.

Critical History and the Future of the PDS

The debate about the health of the Left and the position of the PDS is a prime example of the uncertainty about history in contemporary Germany. The PDS is almost invariably introduced as 'the successor party to the SED'. The point here is not to deny that fact but to ask: which SED? The SED was in fact many parties, even though its public face was monolithic. As we have seen above, behind the façade there were always political and ideological struggles, factions and groups: 110 per centers

---

72. Neugebauer and Stöss, *Die PDS. Geschichte. Organisation. Mitgliederstruktur*, p., 286.

and those with serious reservations.[73] The transition from SED to PDS was therefore bound to involve the public exposure and declaration of factional activity that had hitherto been hidden behind the Stalinist discipline of democratic centralism.

In the minds of some, the SED was a monolithic, dictatorial Stalinist party with no redeeming features whatsoever. For others, it was a political and social *Heimat*, the passing of which is still deeply mourned. A more profitable approach, however, is to see it as a complicated political phenomenon which needs to be fully understood in order to see how its continuation, if it is one, in the form of the PDS manifests itself. The debate about Stalinism and social authoritarianism is important in this context in that it is a vessel that contains more than would necessarily appear from the outside. It is not simply about coming to terms with the past in the form in which we are used to discussing with reference to the NSDAP but actually reveals a need on the Left to arrive at a convincing form of coming to terms with the future. In order to do so, it is necessary, as I have pointed out above, to solve the equation between politics and economics.

Of course, the economics/politics divide has a long history in the Western industrialised world. The prime example of this contradiction is the post-1974 British Conservative Party. It has had to wrestle constantly with the contradiction between requiring a libertarian or neo-liberal economic policy of deregulation whilst maintaining social cohesion and stability: hence the tendency within the neo-conservative movement to fall back on various forms of social and moral authoritarianism. Irving Kristol, for example, once defined neo-conservatism thus: '*Homo oeconomicus* + religion + nationalism'.[74]

The Blair government is facing the same dilemma over its stance on social policy, leading it too to be labelled a socially authoritarian government. Equally, the SPD in Germany is confronted with precisely the same problem. However, the social authoritarianism of which New Labour and the SPD are accused has to be seen as a consequence and symptom of an adaptation to neo-liberal rather than a collectivist economic policy. The communitarian physiognomy which social democracy has started to take on in Europe is seen by many on the Left as one not designed to create a form of opposition to the triumph and dominance of the market, but rather as a form of social compliance designed to underpin free-market relations of production.[75] In that sense we can perhaps define

73. Leonhard, *Die Revolution entläßt ihre Kinder*; von Ditfurth, *Ostalgie oder linke Alternative*, p. 102. See also Wolf, *Woher kommt und wohin geht die PDS?*
74. Quoted in Sven-Eric Liedman, 'Neoliberalismus und Neokonservatismus', *Das Argument*, no. 134, July/August, 1982, p. 497.
75. For a recent discussion of the trend back towards certainty and authoritarian thinking on the New Right as well as the communitarian Left, see Thomas Assheuer, 'Rechte Gewalt und Neue Mitte', *Die Zeit*, no. 36, 31 August 2000, p. 38.

New Labour and the *Neue Mitte* (the New Centre) thus: '*Homo-oeconomicus* + moralism + communitarianism'.

The European social democratic Left has made several attempts at creating a new ideological and political basis for the triumph of economics over politics. This started as the New Labour project, was continued in a German form as the *Neue Mitte*, which was followed by the Blair/Schröder paper of 1999 (actually written by Peter Mandelson and Bodo Hombach) entitled 'Europe: The Third Way/*Die Neue Mitte*'.[76] This latter project met with some resistance from within social democracy itself and is being occluded to some extent by Schröder's project of the *Zivile Bürgergesellschaft* (civil bourgeois society).[77] In all of these various approaches, the death of the welfare state and its role in steering the economy in a traditional Keynesian fashion are at least accepted (if not entirely celebrated) and a neo-monetarist stance is taken on economic policy. In the section from Blair/Schröder entitled 'A New Supply-Side Agenda for the Left', the tone is set with the words; 'The task facing Europe is to meet the challenge of the global economy while maintaining social cohesion in the face of real and perceived uncertainty.'[78]

There are those within the SPD, however, who have noted the contradiction here. As Claus Noé, Lafontaine's erstwhile Secretary of State in the Ministry of Finance, points out: 'That makes about as much sense as demanding a "Socialism of the Right". There can be no such thing as a neo-liberalism of the Left.'[79] This sort of comment from the Lafontaine wing of the SPD is almost indistinguishable from the response of the leadership of the PDS from Gysi through to Zimmer. In his response to the Blair/Schröder paper, for example, Gysi (actually Michael Brie and Dieter Klein) writes; 'The "unproblematical functioning" [Blair-Schröder] of the global market is inimical to social justice and ecological action.'[80] In a similar vein, an editorial in *New Left Review* notes Xudong Zhang's claim that 'postmodern tropes in China today ... attract liberal opposition because they reflect the vigour of a still semi-collectivist socio-economic formation and put in question key tenets of prevailing free-market orthodoxy'.[81]

76. Gerhard Schröder and Tony Blair, *Der Weg nach vorne für Europas Sozialdemokraten*, http://www.spd.de/politik/erneuerung/perspektiven/index.htm for German version, http://www.labour.org.uk/views/index.html for the English version.

77. See 'Schröder, die Bürgergesellschaft und die SPD', *Neue Gesellschaft/Frankfurter Hefte*, September 2000, pp. 520–526.

78. Schröder and Blair, *Der Weg nach vorne für Europas Sozialdemokraten*, Section III, p. 5.

79. Claus Noé '"Oskar sieht nicht wortlos zu"' *Die Zeit*, no. 36, 2 September 1999, p. 9.

80. Gregor Gysi, *Gerechtigkeit ist Modern*, http://www.pds-online.de/1/frames/ 12thesen.htm This document itself, however, has been attacked as a capitulation to Blairite modernisation: see Aron Amm, *Socialism Today*, no. 44, January 2000, http://www.socialismtoday.org/44/pds.html

81. Xudong Zhang, 'Postmodernism and Post-Socialist Society: Cultural Politics in China after the "New Era"', *New Left Review* no. 237, September/October 1999, p. 1.

The question is whether it is possible for the Left to accept modernisation in the Blair/Schröder form and yet still remain 'Left'. On a deeper level, there is the question whether globalisation and marketisation are compatible with social justice and solidarity, the basic themes emphasised by the PDS. Neugebauer and Stöss point out this contradiction in a series of surveys of PDS members and voters, coming to the clear conclusion that: 'It is quite simply *the* party of social justice.'[82] Perhaps we could therefore define the politics of the PDS (or East Germany as a whole) in Kristol's terms thus: '*Homo politicus* + social justice + community'.

A commitment to social justice is not necessarily synonymous, however, with socialist values. As Neugebauer and Stöss also point out, many of the social values adhered to by PDS voters are similar to those held by voters of the *Republikaner*: 'The parties may well be very different but their voters, as measured by their social values, are not.'[83] This in turn raises the question as to whether adherence to the conecpt of social justice as the *ne plus ultra* of daily politics is not in its very nature authoritarian.

The reasons for this extensive programmatic and theoretical debate on the Left are myriad, but must be rooted in the fact that the productive basis of society has changed and, along with it, its class characteristics. As Günter Minnerup has argued elsewhere, it is only possible to understand the paradox of the simultaneous strength and weakness of the Left when one accepts that the traditional base of the labour movement has been worn away by the shift in production but that there has never been as large a 'proletariat' as there is today.[84]

Of course, in the West, this proletariat has changed from an industrial to a post industrial one, but a look at the PDS's voters, if not its members, will only serve to show how this newly proletarianised middle class is voting for left-wing parties traditionally associated with old 'proletarian' values. The reason for this is clear. The newly proletarianised middle classes are far more socially atomised and vulnerable than the old proletariat, and yet the models they have for resistance to that very atomisation are derived from a previous, much less socially complicated period. The traditional struggle between labour and capital which gave rise to the workers' movement still exists, and yet the form which it takes has become much more opaque. It is far more difficult to identify who belongs to which class and therefore the old models of identification become that much more important. In addition, the almost complete absence of an indigenous middle class (many of those who do

---

82. Neugebauer and Stöss, *Die PDS. Geschichte. Organisation. Mitgliederstruktur*, pp. 284–285.
83. Ibid., p. 296.
84. Günter Minnerup, 'The PDS and the Strategic Dilemmas of the German Left', in Barker, *The Party of Democratic Socialism in Germany*, pp. 209–220.

exist vote PDS anyway[85]) contributes to the sense of political openness. The issue of class remains central to many people's concerns. Recent surveys have shown that a growing number of people in the West consider themselves to be in either the under- or working class. The figure rose from 24 per cent in 1991 to 33 per cent in 1996 and remained at 31 per cent in 2000. In the East although the figures have fallen from 60 per cent to 59 per cent to 50 per cent respectively, considering that to be working-class in a workers' state brought with it certain social and psychological benefits and in a capitalist state it quite obviously does not, the figure remains high.[86] For those who consider themselves still to be middle-class in both East and West, the level of social insecurity and the fear of dropping down the social scale have also grown.

For this reason, the traditional parties of labour, rather than small socialist groups or Green parties, tend to be the repositories of protest and defence for both the old and the new working classes. Because both the SPD and the KPD/SED were formed in the crucible of an 'Old Labour' struggle between capital and proletariat, these tend to be the parties in Germany most readily identified as oppositional defence organisations. Over time, however, both of the traditional wings of the labour movement became too heavily integrated with the functions of the state and society, removing their confrontational potential. Both the welfare state and the central plan were forms of rule that relied on the preservation of certain forms of production and distribution for explicitly political aims, and it was the SPD and the SED who stood behind those welfare policies. Economic decision making was secondary to political exigencies in both of these models and these hierarchical politics of collectivism were entirely appropriate to a period of private or state-funded productivism.

These state-oriented workers' parties eventually became so enmeshed in their respective social systems that new movements arose to challenge them: in the West, Green parties and, in the East, post-industrial intellectual opposition movements. What characterised both of these new movements during the period of antiquarianism, however, was their almost complete isolation from the working class. Increasingly, concepts of Fordism, productivism and the collectivist values associated with them were described as belonging to the Stalinist period.[87] This was certainly

---

85. In the East, as large a proportion of the self-employed vote PDS (17 per cent). See Brie, *Die PDS im Ost und West*, http://www.pds-online.de/partei/aktuell/0008/brie-studie.pdf. Yvonne Kaufmann also emphasised this point to me in my interview with her.
86. Brie, 'Ist die PDS noch zu Retten?' pp. 15–16.
87. Even Gregor Gysi, in the *Ingolstadt Manifesto*, proclaims the end of industrialism and seems to equate these values with social democratic and Stalinist momumentalism: 'The industrial mode of production, consumerism and the old form of the social state are at an end in Germany.' *Das Ingolstädter Manifest, Presse und Informationsdienst*, Berlin, 1994, p. 6.

the case until the end of Stalinism in the East and welfarism in the West, but the resulting uncertainties have also called into question the power and significance of the new political movements. The Greens are not the radical power they were and the East German intellectual vanguard has disappeared almost completely. It is this constellation of uncertainty which initially led to the resurgence of social democracy in Europe in the mid 1990s, but it is also the inability of social democracy to actually function as a defender of workers' rights which has helped the PDS and other Left parties to consolidate their positions since then.

Some 20 per cent of voters in the ex-GDR turn to the PDS for support in much the same way as workers used to turn to the more radical earlier versions of the SPD and the KPD. For this reason, the existence of some Stalinist and neo-Stalinist, i.e. monumentalist and antiquarian, forces within the party is not necessarily a hindrance. Many more people now identify with the social nature of the GDR than did when the GDR still existed, and they identify with the PDS because of the antiquarian nostalgia which exists within its emphasis on social cohesion. Whether or not the PDS can be both a left-wing campaigning organisation and a repository of the conservative values identified with the GDR is open to doubt, however.

The reason for this uncertainty lies in the fact that the reality of the GDR was, as Niethammer points out below, very different from the one often portrayed in the Western media. The identification with the GDR was, from the late 1960s onwards, never one based on an approval of or support for the political structures of party rule, but on personal material benefit and stable social conditions. 'Identification with the social system in the GDR is based overwhelmingly on positive memories of the day-to-day material benefits and social security. It is not based on its political and ideological structures. This appears to be the case even for many ex-party members.'[88] As that study of workers in Eisenhüttenstadt in 1987 shows, the fading memories of the GDR are those of relatively good living conditions combined with a rejection of the political structures predominant at that time. Historical debates, therefore, are important only in so far as they help to clarify contemporary political positions. What unites all of the groups in the PDS is an apparent determination to maintain political and social imperatives above those of the individual and the economic. This means that the PDS is always going to be attacked as democratically illegitimate simply because it does not necessarily equate democracy with the free market and individualist capitalism. It has to maintain an attachment to at least leftist, if not explicitly Marxist, values because it has a view of democracy which is closer to the original impetus of social democracy, i.e. social control of the economy, rather than economic control of society.

---

88. Lutz Niethammer, Alexander von Plato and Dorthee Wierling, *Die volkseigene Erfahrung. Eine Archäologie des Lebens in der Industrieprovinz der DDR*, Berlin, 1991, p. 63.

The preponderance of these sorts of socio-political imperatives within the PDS is demonstrated, for example, by Lothar Probst when he notes that: 'Just over 50 per cent of PDS members in Rostock consider representative democracy as simply a masked form of the rule of capital, 80 per cent consider it to be only a temporary state formation and only 6 per cent think it is the best possible form of government.'[89] In the eyes of many in the ex-GDR the democratic deficit of the GDR has been replaced with the illusion of democracy in the Federal Republic. So do these statistics and these social attitudes to the past denote a Stalinist or a Marxist position on the part of these members? If one concludes that they are essentially Stalinist, then one also has to say that almost the entire history of the workers' movement in the last two centuries has been proto-Stalinist. Indeed, the idea that representative democracy does not go far enough and that elements of direct democracy are necessary to balance out the power of the capital-owning élite was one of the founding principles of social democracy and still finds many supporters in many mainstream parties of the Left in Europe.

It is for these reasons that Neugebauer and Stöss also come to such ambivalent conclusions in their study of the PDS, in which they describe it as 'a necessary and useful, and yet anachronistic' but also 'potentially superfluous party'.[90] This conclusion reflects very clearly the problems that political scientists have in fitting the party in with political realities. Another reason for the relative confusion about the PDS and its survival and health can also be traced back to the way in which Western political discussion has, since the 1970s, become increasingly emptied of real ideological debate based on historical analysis and theoretical argument. This may be seen by many as a perfectly healthy, normal and even welcome development, but it does mean that politics is analysed in the same way that any other product of the late-capitalist free market is analysed, namely, as an advertising strategy designed to win over what they regard as customers. In this sense, parties and politicians are compared to brands of cars and other consumer goods. Politics is apparently all about a question of the passive 'supply and demand' of political goods. These approaches will always have trouble analysing or even understanding successful left-wing parties which actually ask fundamental questions about the nature of the system rather than just the day-to-day running of that system.

Oskar Niedermayer, for example, confronts difficulties because he bases his whole premise on an analysis which emanates from the 'supply and demand' school of political theory.[91] Equally, Neugebauer and Stöss fall into this trap very early on in their study when they state that:

89. Lothar Probst, 'Die PDS in Rostock. Eine Lokalstudie über die Anatomie einer postkommunistischen Partei', in Barker, *The Party of Democratic Socialism in Germany*, p. 55.

90. Neugebauer and Stöss, *Die PDS. Geschichte. Organisation. Mitgliederstruktur*, p. 299.

91. Oskar Niedermayer, 'Die Stellung der PDS im ostdeutschen Parteiensystem', in Barker, *The Party of Democratic Socialism in Germany*, pp. 18–38.

> Party systems are not only the reflexes of constellations of social conflict and arenas of political struggles in the state-political sphere. Under democratic conditions they are also competing systems in which suppliers (parties) compete with each other for customers (voters). Under these conditions parties are constantly forced to sell their wares (programmes and policies). Suppliers and their products must be of a quality which will satisfy their customers.[92]

This quotation reflects the extent to which politics is increasingly becoming depoliticised. Democracy, in this interpretation, turns into a mere forum for parading the best-dressed candidates, and, although the PDS is perhaps one of the most successful parties in Germany at playing the advertising game, it is clear that it is also interested in systemic rather than merely superficial issues. And it is for this reason, and not because of its genesis in the SED, that several federal states have decided that it should continue to be the subject of surveillance by the Office of Constitutional Protection. The reasons given for this surveillance are that the PDS wishes to introduce more direct democracy, 'a democratisation of democracy', and that it intends to challenge the existing social relations of production even though both of these aims are catered for in specific paragraphs of the German constitution. As Bisky also wrote in his letter to Richard von Weizsäcker; 'With the concept of the "democratisation of democracy" laid out in its 1998 electoral programme, the PDS has made a serious contribution to the debate about the development and strengthening of democratic relations in the Federal Republic.'[93]

At the same time, however, B'90/Die Grünen called for a political debate with the PDS rather than a system of state surveillance and the SPD Minister of the Interior, Otto Schilly, spoke of the need to treat the PDS as a normal constitutional party. It would seem that the PDS is on its way to becoming such a party but that it is also, at present, the last 'ideological' party of the Federal Republic and that this is both its main strength but also potentially its greatest weakness. The fact that it still sees the world through the prism of history, theory and ideology means that it is unique in the German political spectrum. If, however, its debates and theoretical considerations become too divorced from the realities of day-to-day politics, it could lose support as its base members and voters age and die and the two parts of Germany begin to grow together.

The potential of the PDS does not seem to have been undermined at the 2002 election by any of its opponents' political tactics, but by a constellation of conjunctural events. As the government deals with the various crises which will increase tensions between the SPD and the Greens – such as economic and foreign policy issues – however, the PDS will be able to take positions which will increasingly attract support from disenchanted social democratic and Green voters. The greatest opportunity for the PDS, however, lies in the fact that Greens and the SPD have

---

92. Neugebauer and Stöss, *Die PDS. Geschichte. Organisation. Mitgliederstruktur*, p. 27.
93. Bisky et al., *Die PDS*.

accepted defeat in the ideological and socio-economic debate which has always characterised politics in the modern world, namely, that of the issue of class, wealth distribution, ownership patterns and social organisation. Both the SPD and the Greens accept fully the capitalist consensus and are prepared to become fully integrated into the running of a free-market-based economic system in which even the mildly redistributive policies of the Brandt and Schmidt governments would today seem dangerously radical.

The PDS will have to build upon these dissatisfied groups of voters as well as those forces who were oppositional socialists and Marxists within the SED, and who saw their duty as lying in the creation of a socialist party which could rescue the best traditions of the German workers' movement from the clutches of Stalinism. As this group states in the introduction to the commentary:

> What disturbed us about the GDR was not that there was too much socialism but that there was too little. It was also the contradiction between the emancipatory aims which we associated with the GDR and the constant petty regulations, the political repression, the ideological arrogance, the destruction of nature and the underdeveloped economy. For us the conflict within the SED was a struggle for a different, for a democratic, a modern socialism.[94]

94. Gesellschaftsanalyse und politische Bildung e.V. (ed.), *Zur Programmatik der Partei des Demokratischen Sozialismus. Ein Kommentar*, Berlin, 1997, p. 14.

Conclusions

*I*n conclusion, then, we come to a consideration of the future of the German Left after the end of Stalinism in a world which has undergone a second great transformation at least as fundamental as that which Polyani noted in the 1940s. Are the PDS and parties like them capable of responding at all to the structural crises and changes which face us today? The signs for the PDS are mixed. The Berlin state election of 2001 – where the PDS obtained 47.6 per cent of the vote in the Eastern part of Berlin – showed that the PDS still could not be written off as a political force, even though many had tried to do so as early as March 1990. In those early elections in 1990 the PDS had obtained 16.4 per cent of the overall vote and in some areas of the east the vote was as high as 86 per cent.

That result was dismissed as the last gasp of the old functionaries and bureaucrats concerned about their futures in a united Germany, but, although this group certainly makes up a considerable part of both the membership and voters of PDS voters, its relative success could not be solely attributed to this factor in 1990 and certainly not in 2001. Already in 1990 it was becoming evident that attitudes to the GDR itself were not as clear-cut as was assumed at the time and that not everything that the GDR represented was necessarily seen as negative. Fears about the market economy and the end of the stability and security offered by the Honecker regime were as important in many minds – and often in the same minds – as the hopes raised by an opening to the West and the political freedoms that would bring. The PDS, with its slogan of 'a strong opposition for the weak' in 1990, capitalised on these fears.

In 2002 the PDS failed to either jump the 5 per cent hurdle or get the necessary three direct mandates, and yet this was a close-run thing. A few more votes in Berlin and the party would have been back in parliament. Despite having been once again written off as a serious contender since that federal election, the PDS has not disappeared and has even shown signs of a recovery and improvement in its position once again. Although turnout was relatively low – a factor which will have helped the PDS particularly due to its organisational strength and the level of commitment of its voters – the local elections in Branden-burg on 26 October 2002 saw the party increase its vote by 0.4 per cent and become the strongest party in Potsdam (33.8 per cent), Cottbuss (26.8 per cent), and Frankfurt and der Oder (33.9 per cent). This in an election which saw the SPD's vote fall drastically from around 40 per cent four years previously to around 23 per cent at this election.

On the whole, elections in the ex-GDR since 1990 have been char-acterised by a very sensitive balance between freedom and security and the PDS has been the party which has so far been best able to hold together both of those impetuses for many Eastern voters. By voting PDS, many voters are saying that they are happy to have arrived in the Federal Republic but that they have not yet been made to feel that they are fully welcome. In the Berlin elections, the PDS obtained 47.6 per cent of the vote in the east of Berlin and 6.9 per cent in the West. It subsequently went into coalition with the SPD to form the Berlin Senate with its de facto leader, Gregor Gysi, as Economics Senator for a period of about nine months. So, in the ex-front line of the ex-Cold War the ex-Communist Party was once again in government.

Against this has to be set the fact that, at the federal election in October 2002, the PDS narrowly failed to obtain the necessary five per cent of the vote to achieve representation. There were many reasons for this failure. However, although it is undoubtedly the case that the structural factors which had led to and supported the success of the PDS have not disap-peared, the anti-militaristic conjunctural factors which siphoned off some of its support can also be seen to have become a self-fulfilling ordinance. Voters released from the need to vote PDS may not return to the fold. As Zygmunt Bauman puts it in another context 'no episode is safe from its consequences'.[1] However, the relationship between these structural and conjunctural factors is not yet settled. Despite its relative absence from the daily media landscape, the PDS remains an important political player in Eastern Germany. At the time of writing, the SPD's structural adoption of increased market economic mechanisms with Agenda 2010 is already leading to divisions within the labour movement, from which the PDS may profit as the conjunctural impact of the Iraq crisis fades.

What all of the elections since 1990 have shown, however, is that there is the potential for consolidating the structural majority for the Left which was always likely to come about with German unification. As long ago as 1987, I was arguing that the unification of Germany was an unresolved question and that the West German Left was doing itself

1. Zygmunt Bauman, *Liquid Love*, Cambridge, 2003, p. 52.

a disservice by refusing to discuss it.[2] The reasons for arguing thus were that there are three structural factors which contribute to the dominance of the Left in contemporary Germany and which could be further built upon. They are: firstly, the class nature of the population of the GDR; secondly, the relative geographical isolation of the Catholic parties in the south-west of Germany, where their considerable influence over the Catholic working class is itself beginning to wane; and, thirdly, the non-denominational or predominantly Protestant – and therefore more social-democratically oriented – characteristics of voters in the East of Germany.[3]

Given these facts about the demographic situation in Germany then, demographically at least, the Left could only gain from the unification of Germany. The PDS's strength is therefore rooted not only in its regional base but in historical and demographic circumstances. The PDS's roots are in the East German community and it can build on those roots because it recognises that the very concepts of community, regional organisation, local patriotism and GDR nationalism exist entirely in the political and psychological realm and can be mobilised for particular political ends. The CDU and the SPD are potentially at a double disadvantage in the ex-GDR, firstly because they are seen as West German parties and, secondly, because they come across as essentially individualistic post-collectivist entities at a time when the one thing many in the ex-GDR want is a collective identity.

The leadership of the party is fully aware of the fragile nature of electoral support based on such clearly psychological factors and is developing strategies to consolidate its support in the ex-GDR, while also attempting to extend its support in the West by attracting support from radical youth disgruntled with the political trajectory of the SPD and the Greens.[4] This has been partially successful in certain areas where youth and students are concentrated, but the levels of overall support remain low.[5] Given the politico-demographic situation in Germany, however, an increase in support in the West at the 1998 election to just 1.2 per cent was sufficient to give the PDS an overall level of 5.1 per cent, in addition

---

2. See Thompson, *Socialism and the German Question*.
3. A look at the colour of the map of the constituency results from the October 2002 election is a clear example of this trend: http//:www.bundeswahlleiter.de/bundestagswahl2002/deutsch/ergebnis2002/bund_land/btw2002/kru_btw2002.htm.
4. See my interview with André Brie, 'A purely East German alternative is an illusion'; also Peter Thompson and Günter Minnerup, 'The 1994 Elections: A Provisional Assessment', *Debatte* vol. 2, no. 2, 1994.
5. See statistics for 1994 elections in Brie, *Die PDS im Ost und West – Fakten und Argumente statt Vermutungen*. For example, in Kreuzberg at the 1995 Berlin senate elections the PDS gained 5.3 per cent of the vote.

to their four direct mandates in Berlin and their 20 per cent in the ex-GDR as a whole.[6]

The situation after 2002 has been somewhat different, however. At that election, the PDS was deprived of support mainly in the urban areas and amongst its young and educated voters, who increasingly voted SPD and, to a greater degree, Green. They did this in order to give their support to a coalition government which was under threat and which could have been replaced with a Stoiber-led conservative coalition which would undoubtedly have taken a more pro-American line post-11 September. In many ways the PDS suffered at the 2002 election from the same factor which kept the Greens out of the West German parliament in 1980, namely, the Strauss effect. In 1980, the Greens had been winning much support at the local level and were generally perceived to be making a breakthrough at the national level. The choice of Strauss as chancellor candidate in 1980 drove many potential Green voters back into the arms of Schmidt's SPD as the lesser evil. This did not postpone either Schmidt's demise nor the success of the Greens for more than two years. This similarity has to be offset, of course, against the fact that the PDS has already been represented at the national level since 1990 and therefore appears to be on a falling rather than a rising trend.

In fact the situation, looked at historically, is one of fluctuation. As Dan Hough, among others, has pointed out, the PDS fortunes were consistently falling after its initial successes in 1990. It established itself as a successful party on an almost entirely regional basis and its presence at a national level has always been merely a happy side-effect of its regional strength. In 1990, it remained in the federal parliament due to the separate voting systems between the old and the new states, in 1994 it stayed there because it managed to gain more than the minimum of three directly elected constituency MPs and only in 1998 did it manage to obtain more than the 5 per cent required for fractional status and then by only 0.1 per cent. In 2002 the PDS gained two directly elected MPs in Berlin and only missed gaining more by a handful of votes in Berlin Mitte as well as in Rostock and other East German towns. Despite the fact that the *Magdeburg Model* in Saxony-Anhalt – in which the PDS supported a minority SPD government – collapsed in 2002, this was due to a drop in

6. At the 1994 federal election the PDS gained 19.6 per cent in the East and 0.9 per cent in the West, giving it 4.4 per cent overall. Although this was below the 5 per cent normally required for representation in the German Bundestag, the PDS also gained four seats directly elected by the first vote in East Berlin, giving them a proportional 4.4 per cent of the seats in parliament. At the 1995 Berlin senate elections, the PDS became the strongest party in East Berlin, gaining 36.6 per cent of the vote, and the third strongest in Berlin as a whole with 14.7 per cent, ahead of the Greens on 13.2 per cent. Sources: David Conradt et al. (eds), *Germany's New Politics*, German Studies Review, Arizona, 1995; and *Berliner Zeitung*, 22 October 1995.

SPD rather than PDS support. In that sense, the election result of 2002 was not out of the ordinary for the PDS but merely confirmed its regional basis.

If no episode is safe from its consequences, however, the negative blow to the morale of the party and its voters that that election provided will be hard to recover from and has required the party to withdraw into its strongholds both geographically and politically. It has consolidated itself since the election as a regionally based organisation, critical not only of government policies but of the system of government itself. This was, to a certain extent, an inevitable consequence of defeat at the federal level. The question is whether this reconsolidation can allow it to rise from the ashes a second time. The negative factors which led to its defeat in 2002 are largely conjunctural, whereas the factors which might lead to its revival are more structural and are to do with the nature of the socio-economic situation in which Germany now finds itself.

In this context, the question is whether structural all-German economic phenomena and the trend towards increasing job insecurity as well as a relative breakdown of the postwar social contract offer opportunities for the PDS to capitalise on the disaffection brought about by increased job insecurity. André Brie's analysis seems to suggest that this may well be the case in future. He draws the following six conclusions about the current social and electoral situation for the PDS:

1. The social context of the PDS in East Germany is such that it can mobilise support from all sectors of society. In this sense it is a real catch-all party (*Volkspartei*).
2. The electoral bases of its support in East and West Germany are clearly differentiated. In the West it speaks to not only the socially heterogeneous groups who have emigrated from the East but also (a) primarily young voters, (b) parts of the critical intelligentsia and (c) (since 1998) sectors of society negatively affected by economic 'modernisation' and the socially disadvantaged.
3. Since 1990, there has been a gradual levelling upwards in many areas of society. This also applies to social composition. However, there remain significant social divisions.
4. There is a tendency towards a higher level of education and sympathy for the PDS. The vote amongst those with *Abitur* (A levels) and university degrees is significantly higher (around twice as high) than in other social layers
5. The proportion of PDS votes increases with the degree of urbanisation whilst, at the same time, the relatively weak position in rural areas has also been overcome.

6. Support for the PDS is particularly marked among white-collar workers and civil servants, the intelligentsia, those with *Abitur*, students, the unemployed (which, however, is connected with the social composition of the unemployed in East Germany), the non-religious and members of trades unions.[7]

Dietmar Wittich, on the other hand, has pointed out that since 2000 the PDS has started to lose vital support amongst precisely those groups where it has traditionally been strongest: the young, those in education, those with a degree, civil servants generally, the self-employed and the religiously non-aligned.[8] Added to that, the reduced profile of the party as a result of Gysi's retreat from a leading role and its relative lack of experience at local and national level has seriously undermined the PDS in the past two years.[9]

The disunity which is indeed apparent in Germany is, therefore as much a product of the Disraelian idea of two nations in one state as it is of the geographically and geo-strategically divided one with which we are perhaps more preoccupied. Walter Ulbricht once famously described this as a Germany divided between the Krupps (the wealthy industrialists) and the Krauses (the ordinary workers). Germany's real problem is that the socio-economic and the historic-geographic division of Germany overlap to a very high degree and the proletarian nature of the ex-GDR is underpinned by the re-emergence of class as a central dynamic. Its relative vulnerability to the vagaries of the economic forces at work in Europe at present appears to cement divisions and disunities in place which in fact have little to do with either the GDR or the Federal Republic. The concentration of heavy industry in the ex-GDR for reasons of political and social necessity rather than economic efficiency means that the collapse of those industries brought not only economic dislocation but considerable psychological disruption as well. At least in the West people were largely aware that redundancy and unemployment were a possibility, in the East the brutality of economic reality has come as something of a shock. The apparent 'untouchability' of the PDS by both the SPD and the Greens/Alliance '90 has now largely disappeared as the Magdeburger Model in Sachsen-Anhalt and participation in government in Mecklenburg-Vorpommern and now, since January 2002, in Berlin have shown.

The problem facing the PDS in the coming months and years will be very similar to that encountered by the SPD itself before its 'conversion' to the acceptance of market capitalist social relations and Western integration. It should be remembered that until the Godesberg Programme of

7. See Brie, *Die PDS im Ost und West – Fakten und Argumente statt Vermutungen*, p. 17.
8. Brie, 'Ist die PDS noch zu Retten?'
9. In 2002, 78 per cent of voters in the East and 71 per cent in the West gave Gysi's resignation as a major reason for not voting PDS, ibid, p. 26.

1959 the SPD too was regarded by many as a dangerously left-wing proto-Marxist party that could not be trusted with power. Before one concludes from this, however, that the PDS needs to undertake its own Bad Godesberg before it can be fully rehabilitated, three factors need to be considered which would prevent it from doing so.

Firstly, by 1959 the SPD was the only party representing the Left in West Germany. It had no need to worry about competing on the same political ground as any other party. Secondly, Germany and the whole of the Western world found itself on a long upward wave of economic prosperity in which growth and profit rates rose continually and unemployment fell away consistently throughout the 1950s. Capitalism seemed indeed triumphant and the requirement for a political campaign against a supposedly exploitative system which was in fact apparently bringing prosperity to everyone was made redundant. The dynamic of global society at that time was in any case towards social-democratisation and a shift to the Left. The SPD only had to shift slightly to the right, indeed only to unify its programmatic demands with the reality of its political positions and actions, and it became 'fit for government'. Thirdly, the Long Cold War between capitalism and Stalinism had frozen political debate into a sterile struggle over bloc loyalty which removed any possibility of workers' unity in the two German states.

All three of these conditions have now changed fundamentally.

Firstly, the PDS has to compete with both the SPD and the Greens and can only do so by retaining a distinctive left-wing and Marxist profile. A critique of some of the PDS leadership's moves towards social-democratisation has come from the SPD in the form of an article entitled 'Forwards to Marx!' in which Peter von Oertzen states that historical self-criticism was all well and good but the PDS should not fall back on 'outdated social democratic or even social-liberal models'.[10] Rather it would be better off turning to the traditions of Anarcho-Syndicalism. He maintains that 'a marked tendency towards Marxism and the traditions of revolutionary socialism of all kinds is highly desirable'.[11]

Secondly the 1950s and early 1960s period represented the high point of the 'politicisation' of economics and the subordination of the market to social demands. In that sense, Bad Godesberg represented convergence rather than capitulation. Today, the situation is reversed. Economics are now dominant and are dragging politics back towards the position of a servant to the demands of international capital. Social democratic parties in power today are forced to capitulate to this dynamic. This means that the PDS has to maintain an anti-capitalist edge to its policies to remain distinctive.

10. Peter von Oertzen, 'Zu wünschen: Hinwendung "Vorwärts zu Marx"', *Neues Deutschland*, 17 January 1997, p. 3.
11. Ibid.

Thirdly, the end of the Long Cold War and division of Germany has brought with it the end of the division of the German working class. Although that class has changed and the proletarianisation of the new middle classes continues apace, this dynamic brings with it opportunities for the PDS to profile itself as the defender of collective interests in all fields of society. It has also enabled socialist and Marxist thought to be liberated from the strait-jackets of NATO social democracy and Stalinist monumentalism and antiquarianism.

Even though the new Basic Programme which was adopted at the Chemnitz Congress in late October 2002 – and which was hailed by *Der Spiegel* as the PDS's 'Bad Godesberg' – speaks of a new acceptance of competition, the profit motive and entrepreneurialism as dynamic economic motors, this cannot really be compared to the wholesale dismissal of socialism and socialist measures involved in the SPD's transition in the late 1950s. The Bisky-Brie-Gysi group have certainly been successful in reforming the PDS's approach to economics – and in a period of the primacy of economics this should not come as a surprise – but the rest of the programme recognises the need to both maintain an Eastern focus and to establish an identity which positions it clearly on and to the left of German social democracy. Equally, the contention in the preamble to this new programme that the party condemns all crimes committed by the GDR state between 1949 and 1989 is not the great departure that the media have presented it as. The PDS, in its majority, has always recognised that the dictatorial elements of the SED's rule in the GDR were indefensible. Its main difficulty, however, resided in the fact that to criticise those crimes was to appear to criticise the GDR *in toto*, something which the bulk of membership of the PDS would not find so easy to tolerate. The PDS is perhaps finally finding a way to unpack its own rucksack without discarding all of its contents regardless of their value.

In conclusion, therefore, we can say that it is not that the ex-GDR and therefore also the PDS, are primarily victims of their own history but that they have become victims of everybody's present. We all experience disunity within our own lives and societies, whether it is between classes or races or nations or regions or genders but the disunity is usually a socio-historical rather than an essentialist one. Truth is not in that sense decentred but merely disrupted. Class, racial, national, regional or gender disunification is a characteristic of the modern age and its possible transcendence is therefore to be located in much larger questions than simply those of problems of communication between East and West Germans.[12]

12. The Election result in Sachsen-Anhalt on 26 April 1998, in which the DVU obtained 13 per cent of the vote and the CDU was reduced to 22 per cent, giving a structural majority to the Left parties (even though they were unable to form a government), was a first indication of the way in which class conflict returned to the German political stage some ten years after the fall of the wall.

The fundamental question now facing the PDS and all other parties is whether there can be local solutions to global problems. The more that globalisation of the economy takes hold, the more there are temptations to try and control its consequences at a local level. The PDS as a regional party with state governmental responsibility is trying to administer psychological first aid to local communities which have been damaged by global trends. These trends have been at work in the world for far longer than the term globalisation has been in use and their worst effects have probably not yet been fully realised, particularly in Germany. The PDS's response to this crisis is twofold. On the one hand, it attempts to act as a social defence organisation, helping local communities to at least speak out about the effects of unification. At the same time, however, it has to try to be a party which puts the episodic nature of German unification into some sort of structural perspective and to show that it was merely a symptom of a wider global *Wende*. The two elements have to go together in order for the PDS to survive. If it attempts to survive simply as a defence organisation at the local level, it will be forced into the position of having to administer the social ravages of a globalised free market. Indications are that this is already the case, with PDS votes falling furthest in those East German states where they are in government, such as Mecklenburg-Vorpommern. If, however, the party simply attempts to become a radical oppositional movement, then it risks losing the support of those who look to it for defence and responsibility and who indeed vote for it precisely for those reasons.

The problem is that, if there are no local solutions to global problems, then the fall of communism and the end of the concept of socialism imply that there are equally no global solutions to local problems. Socialism essentially understood and continues to understand itself as providing the global answer to individual and localised problems. In that sense it is, by its very nature, a totalising approach. This is the real nub of the PDS's electoral problems: the impression that the neo-liberal Americanisation of the economy is irresistible, that history has indeed ended and that resistance is futile. However, the PDS has no option other than to attempt to mobilise resistance from its power base in the East and its potential in the West. A survey in 2001 showed that the potential is there. Over 20 per cent of Western Germans and around 50 per cent of Eastern Germans described themselves as 'pro-socialist and anti-capitalist'. In addition, many of those who described themselves as in the centre of politics were also in favour of 'fundamental social change, more democracy and had a positive attitude to socialist ideas'.[13] The PDS will inevitably become trapped in the contradictions of regionalism if it does not attempt to maintain at least aspirations towards global solutions and to mobilise this 'coalition of the willing' for social change and security. Regionalism

13. Chrapa and Wittich, 2001, in Brie, 'Ist die PDS noch zu Retten?', p. 25.

requires no more than administrative competence and a readiness to carry the blame for inevitable failure rather as the SED did in 1989. This is not, however, simply a matter of ideological shadow-boxing within the PDS itself. It is based in a changing world and the political consequences that change brings with it.

As Polanyi maintained in *The Great Transformation*, the disembedded economy is, in the long term, an impossibility.[14] The movement towards an unregulated market-state is a conscious and planned political programme designed to reinstate the absolute primacy of economics. He also pointed out that the last century was characterised – both positively and negatively – by conflict created by spontaneous social reactions to that plan. Fascism and Stalinism issued out of the struggle for social control over the economy. Today we find ourselves in a similar situation. The disembedded economy is once again worshipped but the social reactions to it are as yet still in their embryonic and unconscious forms. In order for the PDS to survive, it must be prepared to take a role in the re-establishment of the primacy of politics and to lead a return to the critical tradition of the international workers' movement.

14. Karl Polanyi, *The Great Transformation*, Boston, 2001

BIBLIOGRAPHY

Alt, H. *Die Stellung des Zentralkomitees der SED im politischen System der DDR.* Cologne, 1987.

Amis, M. *Koba the Dread: Laughter and the Twenty Million*, London, 2002.

Amm, A. *Socialism Today*, no. 44, January 2000, http://www.socialismtoday.org/44/pds.html.

Assheuer, T. 'Rechte Gewalt und Neue Mitte', *Die Zeit* no. 36 (31 August 2000): 38.

Barker, P. ed. *The Party of Democratic Socialism in Germany. Modern Post-Communism or Nostalgic Populism?* Amsterdam and Atlanta, 1998.

Bauman, Z. *Liquid Love*, Cambridge, 2003

Behrend, H., ed. *Die Abwicklung der DDR. Wende und Wiedervereinigung von innen gesehen.* Frankfurt, 1996.

———— 'Bürgerbewegungen in der DDR und danach – Aufstieg, Niedergang und Vermächtnis', *Hintergrund* no. 3 (1997): 16–35.

Berg, S. *Das lange Leben der DDR. Ostdeutsche zwischen Emanzipation und Nationalismus.* Berlin, 1995.

Biedenkopf, K. 'The Transition Process in Germany and Its Relevance for Europe', http://www.worldbank.org/wbi/lectures/bieden-text.html.

Bisky, L. et al. *Rücksichten. Politische und juristische Aspekte der DDR- Geschichte.* Hamburg, 1993.

———— Heuer, U. and Schumann, M. *'Unrechtsstaat'? Politische Justiz und die Aufarbeitung der DDR- Vergangenheit.* Hamburg, 1994.

———— *Wut im Bauch. Kampf um die PDS. 29. November bis 7. Dezember 1994. Erlebnisse – Dokumente – Chronologie.* Berlin, 1995.

———— et al. *Die PDS – Herkunft und Selbstverständnis.* Berlin, 1996.

———— et al. *Unmittelbare Demokratie zwischen Anspruch und Wirklichkeit. Kolloquium der PDS-Fraktion im Landtag Brandenburg zum 5. Jahrestag der Landesverfassung am 13.09.1997.* Berlin, 1998.

———— and Gysi, G. *An unserem Wirken wollen wir gemessen werden.* Pressedienst, 1998/33, http://www.pds-online.de/geschichte/9808/weizsaecker-brief.htm.

———— and Gysi, G. 'Mit demokratischen Mitteln die politischen und sozialen Menschenrechte verteidigen. Brief an den ex-Bundespräsidenten Richard von Weizsäcker', Pressedienst PDS, no. 33, 14 August 1998

Bobbit, *The Shield of Achilles. War, Peace and the Course of History* London, 2002.

Bogisch, F. 'Die PDS ist ein ernsthafter politischer Partner', *Die Neue Gesellschaft/Frankfurter Hefte* vol. 44, no. 4 (1997): 357–359.

Bollinger, S. et al. *Die DDR Kann nicht über Stalins Schatten springen. Reformen im Kalten Krieg – SED zwischen NÖS und Prager Frühling.* Berlin, 1993.

_____ *Dritter Weg zwischen den Blöcken? Prager Frühling 1968: Hoffnung ohne Chance: mit einem Anhang bisher nicht veröffentlichter Dokumente zur Haltung der SED-Führung zum Prager Frühling.* Berlin, 1995.

_____ *Konflikte, Krisen und politische Stabilität in der DDR: Gedanken zur historischen Unfähigkeit eines realsozialistischen Konfliktmanagements.* Berlin, 1996.

_____ *Vielfalt sozialistischen Denkens.* Berlin, 1998.

_____ *1989 – eine abgebrochene Revolution: verbaute Wege nicht nur zu einer besseren DDR?* Berlin, 1999.

_____ *DDR-Geschichte. Nostalgie oder Totalkritik?* Berlin [no date given].

Bortfeldt, H. *Von der SED zur PDS – Aufbruch zu neuen Ufern? Sommer-Herbst 1989 – 18. Marz 1990.* Berlin, 1990.

Brandt, P. and Ammon, H. *Die Linke und die nationale Frage*, Reinbeck bei Hamburg, 1981

_____ and _____ H. *Die Deutsche Einheit kommt bestimmt*, Bergisch Gladbach, 1982

Brenner, R. 'The Economics of Global Turbulence'. *New Left Review* no. 229, 1998.

Breuer, Rolf-E. 'Die fünfte Gewalt. Herrscht die Wirtschaft über die Politik? Nein! Aber freie Finanzmärkte sind die wirkungsvollste Kontrollinstanz staatlichen Handels', *Die Zeit*, no. 18, 2000: 21–22.

Brie, A. 'Die PDS weiss nicht, wohin sie will', *taz* 16 August 1996.

_____ et al. *Zur Programmatik der Partei des Demokratischen Sozialismus. Ein Kommentar.* Berlin 1997.

_____ *Die PDS im Ost und West – Fakten und Argumente statt Vermutungen.* Berlin, 2000. http://www.pds-online.de/partei/aktuell/0008/brie-studie.pdf.

Brie, M. *Die PDS – Strategiebildung im Spannungsfeld von gesellschaftlichen Konfliktlinien und politischer Identität.* Berlin, 2000.

_____ 'Ist die PDS noch zu Retten?' *RLS standpunkte* no. 3, 2003, http://www.rosaluxemburgstiftung.de/Stiftung/Uebersicht/Satzung/index.htm

_____ and Klein, D. *Der Engel der Geschichte. Befreiende Erfahrungen einer Niederlage.* Berlin, 1993.

_____ and Woderich, R., eds. *Die PDS im Parteiensystem.* Berlin, 2000.

_____, Herzig, M., and Koch, T. *Postkommunistische Kaderorganisation, ostdeutscher Traditionsverein oder linke Volkspartei? Empirische Befunde und kontroverse Analysen.* Cologne, 1995.

Campbell of Alloway, Hansard, 22 January 1997, column 742.

Castells, M. *The Rise of the Network Society.* Cambridge, Mass. and Oxford, 1996.

Chronik der PDS 1989–1997, Berlin, 1998.

Conradt, D. et al., eds. *Germany's New Politics. Parties and Issues in the 1990s.* Arizona, 1995.

Ralf Dahrendorf, 'Die globale Klasse und die neue Ungleichheit', *Merkur, Deutsche Zeitschrift für euopäisches Denken*, Stuttgart, no. 11, 2000, 1057–1068.

Dau, R. *Gemeinschaft oder Gesellschaft? Fragen an das gesellschaftstheoretische Erbe von Marx.* Berlin, 1995.

Davis, M. 'Planet of Slums. Urban Involution and the informal Proletariat' in *New Left Review* vol. 26, 2004, 5–34.

Day, R. 'The Theory of the Long Cycle: Kondratiev, Trotsky, Mandel', *New Left Review* no. 99, 1976, 67–82.

Deinert, R-G. *Institutionenvertrauen, Demokratiezufriedenheit und Extremwahl. Ein Vergleich zwischen westdeutscher Rechts- und ostdeutscher PDS-Wahl.* St Augustin, 1997.

Der schwere Weg der Erneuerung – Von der SED zur PDS. Eine Dokumentation. Berlin, 1990.

Dieckmann, C. 'Bitte nicht Aussteigen!', *Die Zeit* no. 40, 28 September 2000, 3.

―――― *Temperatursprung. Deutsche Verhältnisse.* Frankfurt, 1995.

―――― 'Stalins Schädelstätte der 20 Millionen in seinen Lagern Ermordeten ist das Golgotha der Utopie', *Die Zeit*, 43, 19 October 2000, 11.

Die Linke und die 'soziale Frage'. Wie rechte Wahlerfolge, Nationalismus und Rassismus zusammenhängen, http://www.nadir.org/nadir/periodika/bahamas/auswahl/web40.htm.

Die Neue'ste. Links, wo das Herz ist – PDS. Berlin, 1990.

von Dohnanyi, K. 'Gemeinsin und Zivilcourage. Die Vergangenheit in der Zukunft Deutschlands', *Merkur* no. 11 (2000), 68.

Dönhoff, M. 'Die deutsche Leitkultur', *Die Zeit*, 9 November 2000, 4.

'"Die Duldung der rechstextremen Szene in der DDR ist zu verurteilen"', an interview with Lothar Bisky, *Der Tagesspiegel* 3 November 1998, 16.

Eissel, D. 'Distribution Policy in the Kohl Era', *Debatte*, vol. 7, no. 1, 1999.

Elster, J. *Logic and Society: Contradictions and Possible Worlds*, Chichester, 1978.

Engels, F. 'Antwort an die Redaktion der Sächsischen Arbeiter-Zeitung', Marx-Engels, *Werke*, vol. 22, Berlin, DDR, 1972, 68–70.

Everts, C. *Politscher Extremismus. Theorie und Analyse am Beispiel der Parteien REP und PDS.* Berlin, 2000.

Faulenbach, B. et al., *Die Partei hatte immer recht. Aufarbeitung von Geschichte und Folgen der SED-Diktatur in Deutschland*, Essen, 1994.

Falkner, T. and Huber, D. eds, *Aufschwung PDS. Rote Socken zurück zur Macht?* Munich, 1994.

Fehrle, B. 'Mißverständnisse mit Brie. Der Parteivorstand ist nur scheinbar einer Meinung', *Berliner Zeitung*, 27 August 1996, http://www.berlinonline.de/wissen/berliner_zeitung/archiv/1996/0827/politik/0031/.

Foschepoth, J. ed., *Kalter Krieg und Deutsche Frage.* Göttingen and Zürich, 1985.

―――― *Adenauer und die Deutsche Frage.* Göttingen and Zürich, 1988.

Fritsch-Bournazel, R. *Europa und die deutsche Einheit.* Bonn, 1990.

Fulbrook, M. *Anatomy of Dictatorship Inside the GDR.* Oxford, 1995.

―――― *Interpretations of the Two Germanies. 1945–1990.* Basingstoke, 2000.

Fukuyama, F. *The End of History and the Last Man.* London and New York, 1992.

Gerhardt, S. *Politbürokratie und Hebelwirtschaft in der DDR. Zur Kritik einer moralischen Ökonomie.* Berlin, 1997.

Gesellschaftsanalyse und politische Bildung e.V. (ed.), *Zur Programmatik der Partei des Demokratischen Sozialismus. Ein Kommentar*, Berlin, 1997.

Getrennte Vergangenheit, gemeinsame Zukunft, 4 vols, Munich, 1997.

Gorz, A. *Farewell to the Working Class: an essay on Post-industrial Socialism*, London, 1982.

Gowan, P. *The Global Gamble*. London, 1999.

Greffrath, M. 'Weder Dschungel noch Zoo. Nur in der Verteidigung des Sozialstaates kann Europa seine politische Identität finden', *Die Zeit* 9 November (2000): 13.

Gysi, G. *Gerechtigkeit ist Modern* at http://www.pds-online.de/1/frames/12thesen.htm.

――― *Einspruch!* Berlin, 1992.

――― *Das war's noch lange nicht*. Düsseldorf, 1997.

――― 'Nach neuen Wegen Suchen', *Der Spiegel* no. 40 (1999): 61.

Habermas, J. *Die Neue Unübersichtlichkeit. Kleine Politische Schriften*, Frankfurt, 1985.

Halliday, F. *The Making of the Second Cold War*. London, 1983.

Harich, W. *Keine Schwierigkeiten mit der Wahrheit*. Berlin, 1993.

Haug, W.F. and Haug, F., eds. *Unterhaltungen über den Sozialismus nach seinem Verschwinden*. Berlin, 2002.

Henrich, R. *Der vormundschaftliche Staat. Vom Versagen des real existierenden Sozialismus*. Reinbeck bei Hamburg, 1989.

Herbst, A., Stephan, G. and Winckler, J. *Die SED. Geschichte-Organisation-Politik. Ein Handbuch*. Berlin, 1997.

Herrnstadt, R. *Das Herrnstadt-Dokument. Das Politbüro der SED und die Geschichte des 17. Juni 1953*. Reinbeck bei Hamburg, 1990.

Heuer, U.-J. *Die Rechtsordnung der DDR. Anspruch und Wirklichkeit*. Baden-Baden, 1995.

――― ed. *Marxismus und Demokratie*. Baden-Baden, 1989.

――― and Riege, G. *Der Rechtsstaat – eine Legende? Erfahrungen zweier Rechtswissenschaftler 1990/91 in Volkskammer und Bundestag*. Baden-Baden, 1992.

――― and ―――, eds. *Neues Deutschland – Neue Verfassung?* Bonn, 1992.

――― and Werner, H. *Gegenmacht: Demokratie. Demokratiserung gegen Macht*. Berlin, 1994.

――― and Wolf, W. *Weltanschauung und Linke*. Cologne, 1995.

―――, ――― and ――― *Sozialistisches Ziel und praktische Politik*. Cologne, 1996.

―――, ――― and ――― *Die Sozialisten und die Machtfrage heute*. Cologne, 1997.

Heuser, Uwe Jean. 'In den Zeiten der Wirtschaft. Die Neue Begeisterung für die Ökonomie', *Die Zeit* no. 44, 2000, 1.

Hilsberg, S. 'Strategien gegen die PDS', *Die Neue Gesellschaft/Frankfurter Hefte* vol. 43, no. 10 (1996): 921–925.

Hobsbawm, E. *Age of Extremes. The Short Twentieth Century 1914–1991*, London, 1995.

Hough, D. *The Fall and Rise of the PDS in Eastern Germany*. Birmingham, 2002 http://www.mysan.de/article1542.html/

Husson, M. 'Riding the Long Wave', *historical materialism* no. 5 (1999): 77–102.

Das Ingolstädter Manifest, Presse und Informationsdienst, Berlin, 1994.

Jarausch, K., ed. *Dictatorship as Experience. Towards a Socio-Cultural History of the GDR*. New York and Oxford, 1999.

Joffe, J. 'Deutschland – das Ende der Eiszeit', *Die Zeit* no. 15 (2000): 3.

――― 'Revolte Rückwärts', *Die Zeit*, no. 18 (2003): 1.

Johnson, C. 'Die Rolle eines Ersatz-Rom', *Der Spiegel* no. 45 (2000): 254.

Jünger, E. and Schmitt, C. *Briefwechsel*, Stuttgart, 1999.

Klein, D. 'Den Marktmechanismus planvoll nutzen? Eine Reformperspektive für die blockierte Gesellschaft (with W. Brüggen/T. Westphal)', *Blätter für deutsche und internationale Politik* no. 10 (1998).

―――― Moderne, Modernisierung und PDS. PDS: Schriften zur Diskussion. Berlin 2000

―――― Globalisierung und Standort Deutschland. Unausweichliche Handlungszwänge á la Marx oder Gestaltungsfreiräume in Anknüpfung an Marx? In: Volker Gerhardt (ed.) *Marxismus. Versuch einer Bilanz*. Magdeburg 2001

Koch, M. 'Kein kommunistischer Noske', *Neues Deutschland* 7 November (1998): 15.

Kosing, A. *Nation in Geschichte und Gegenwart*. Berlin, 1976.

Kunert, G. 'Der verschlagene Biedermann', *Der Spiegel* no. 37 (1999).

Land, R. and Possekel, R. *Fremde Welten. Die gegensätzliche Deutung der DDR durch SED-Reformer und Bürgerbewegung in den 80er Jahren*. Berlin, 1998.

Lang, J. *Das Prinzip Gegenmacht. PDS und Parlamentarismus*. Konrad-Adenauer-Stiftung. Reihe: Interne Studien und Berichte no. 166 (1998).

―――― and Moreau, P. *PDS. Das Erbe der Diktatur*. Munich, 1994.

――――, Moreau, P. and Neu, V. *Auferstanden aus Ruinen...? Die PDS nach dem Superwahljahr 1994*. Bonn-Bad Godesberg, 1995.

Leeder, K. *Breaking Boundaries. A New Generation of Poets in the GDR*. Oxford, 1996.

Liedman, S.-E. 'Neoliberalismus und Neokonservatismus', *Das Argument* no. 134 (1982): 495–503.

Löwy, M. *The Politics of Combined and Uneven Development. The Theory of Permanent Revolution*, London, 1981.

Malycha, A. *Partei von Stalins Gnaden? Die Entwicklung der SED zur 'Partei neuen Typs' in den Jahren 1946 bis 1950*. Berlin, 1996.

Mandel, E. *Late Capitalism*, London, 1975.

Marx-Engels, *Werke*, vol. 3, Berlin, DDR, 1969.

――――, *Werke*, vol. 8, Berlin, DDR, 1972.

――――, *Werke*, vol. 22, Berlin, DDR, 1972.

Mayer, H. *Nur eine Partei nach Stalins Muster? Weichenstellungen für die SED im Jahre 1948*. Berlin,1998.

Mergel, T. and Welskopp, T. (eds), *Geschichte Zwischen Kultur und Gesellschaft. Beiträge zur Theoriedebatte*, Munich, 1997.

Minnerup, G. 'The Bundesrepublik Today', *New Left Review* no. 99, 1976, 3–46.

―――― 'The PDS and Strategic Dilemmas of the Left'. In: *The Party of Democratic Socialism in Germany. Modern Post-Communism or Nostalgic Populism?*, Amsterdam and Atlanta, 1998, 209–220.

Moreau, *PDS. Anatomie einer postkommunistischen Partei*. Bonn, 1992.

―――― *Gefahr von links? Die PDS auf dem Weg zur Etablierung*. Wiesbaden, 1994.

―――― *Was will die PDS?* Berlin, 1994.

―――― 'Aufbruch zu neuen Ufern? Zustand und Perspektiven der PDS', *aus politik und zeitgeschichte* vol. 46, no. 6 (1996): 54–61.

Moreau, P. and Lang, J.-P. *Linksextremismus. Eine unterschätzte Gefahr?* Bonn, 1996.

Naimark, N.M. *The Russians in Germany. A History of the Soviet Zone of Occupation, 1945-1949*. Cambridge Mass. and London, 1997.

Neubert, E. *Geschichte der Opposition in der DDR 1949-1989*, Berlin, 1998.

Neugebauer, G. and Stöss, R. *Die PDS. Geschichte. Organisation. Mitgliederstruktur.* Opladen, 1996.

Nietzsche, F. *Werke und Briefe*. Munich, 2000.

Nolte, E. *Der europäische Bürgerkrieg 1917-1945. Nationalsozialismus und Bolschewismus*. Munich, 1997

OECD, *Social Expenditure 1960-1985*, Paris, 1985.

Oelßner, F. *Rosa Luxemburg*. Berlin, 1951.

Peters, A. 'Reparations-Ausgleichs-Plan', *Blatter für deutsche und internationale Politik* no. 1 (1990).

Podewin, N. *Ulbrichts Weg and die Spitze der Macht. Stationen zwischen 1945 und 1954*. Berlin, 1998.

Polanyi, K. *The Great Transformation*, Boston, 2001.

Programm der PDS. Berlin, 1994.

Prokop, S. *Ein Streiter für Deutschland. Auseinandersetzungen mit Wolfgang Harich.* Berlin, 1996.

Rehberg J. *WTO/GATT Research* http://www.llrx.com/features/wto.htm#WTO/GATT Legal Instruments

Ross, C. *The East German Dictatorship. Problems and Perspectives in the Interpretation of the GDR*. London, 2002.

Schirdewan, K. *Aufstand gegen Ulbricht*. Berlin, 1994.

'Schnell ans Meer', *Der Spiegel* no. 47 (1995): 50.

Schröder, G. and Blair, T. *Der Weg nach vorne für Europas Sozialdemokraten*, http://www.spd.de/politik/erneuerung/perspektiven/index.htm

Schröder, R. 'SED, PDS und die Republik', *Die Neue Gesellschaft/Frankfurter Hefte* vol. 43, no. 10 (1996): 912-921.

Segert, D. 'Was war die DDR? Schnitte durch ihr politisches System', *Berliner Debatte INITIAL* vol. 9, nos. 2/3 (1998): 5-22.

Sloterdijk, *Critique of Cynical Reason*, London and New York, 1988.

Statute of the PDS (1991 and 1997 versions): http://www.pds-online.de/partei/dokumente/statut/.

Staud, T. 'Auf dem Weg zur CSU des Ostens', *Die Zeit* no. 43, 19 October (2000): 6.

Staud, T. 'Ossis sind Türken' *Die Zeit* no. 41, 1 October (2003): 9.

Streisand, J. *Deutsche Geschichte von den Anfängen bis zur Gegenwart. Eine marxistische Analyse*, Cologne, 1976.

Sturm, E. *'Und der Zukunft zugewandt'? Eine Untersuchung zur 'Politfähigkeit' der PDS*. Opladen, 2000.

Thompson, *Socialism and the German Question*. Unpublished dissertation, Portsmouth Polytechnic, 1987.

_____ 'The GDR Election', *PASGAS* vol. 2, no. 3 (1990): 81-91.

_____ 'The German Question', *PASGAS* vol. 2, no. 3 (1990): 98-108.

_____ 'Progress, Reason and the End of History', *History of European Ideas* vol. 18, no.4, (1994): 21-31.

_____ 'Shutting the stable door', *Times Higher Education Supplement* 6 May (1994): 19.

———— 'The 1994 Elections: A Provisional Assessment', *Debatte* vol. 2, no.2 (1994).

———— '"A purely East German Alternative is an Illusion" Interview with André Brie, election manager of the PDS', *Debatte* vol. 2, no. 2 (1994).

———— 'Long Waves and Social Authoritarianism. A Study of the PDS'. In: *Mutual Exchanges: Sheffield-Münster Colloquium*, vol. 1, Frankfurt, 1998, 242–257.

———— 'Jorg Haider and the Paradoxical Crisis of Social Democracy in Europe Today', *Debatte* vol. 8, no. 1 (2000): 9–22.

———— 'Jörg Haider, Tony Blair und der Wirtschaftsliberalismus', *Berliner Debatte INITIAL* no. 4 (2000): 93–101.

———— 'The PDS. Marx's Baby or Stalin's Bathwater?'. In: *Rückblick und Revision: Die DDR im Spiegel der Enquete-Kommision*. Amsterdam, 2000.

———— 'The PDS: "CSU des Ostens"? – Heimat and the Left'. In: *Recasting German Identity. Culture Politics and Literature in the Berlin Republic*. Rochester, 2002, 123–141.

———— 'The Primacy of Politics – Interview with Gregor Gysi', *Debatte* vol. 3, no. 1 (2002) 25–31.

Tylecote, A. *The Long Wave in the World Economy. The Present Crisis in Historical Perspective*, London, 1992.

von Ditfurth, C. *Ostalgie oder linke Alternative?. Meine Reise durch die PDS*. Cologne, 1998.

von Oertzen, P. 'Zu wünschen: Hinwendung "Vorwärts zu Marx"', *Neues Deutschland*, 17 January 1997, 3.

Weber, H. *Aufbau und Fall einer Diktatur*, Cologne, 1991.

Weisskirchen, G. 'Innere und äußere Zivilisierung. Die Opposition in der DDR und in Osteuropa'. In: Faulenbach, B. et al. *Die Partei hatte immer recht. Aufarbeitung von Geschichte und Folgen der SED-Diktatur in Deutschland*, Essen, 1994, 189.

Welker, P. ed. *Die Sache mit der Nation 1. Nachdenken über ein für Linke schwieriges Thema. Materialien zweier Fachtagungen 9.Mai 1993, 27 November 1993*, Berlin, 1994.

Wolf, H. *Woher kommt und wohin geht die PDS?* Berlin, 1995.

Wolf, W. 'PDS-Deutschtümelei. Kann es einen "linken Patriotismus" geben? Eine Antwort auf Klaus Höpcke', *Junge Welt*, 4 November 2000.

World Bank, World Development Report, 1981, 135. Quoted by Ted Grant, 'Russia: From Revolution to Counterrevolution', http://easyweb.easynet.co.uk/~socappeal/russia/part6.html

Zhang, X. 'Postmodernism and Post-Socialist Society: Cultural Politics in China after the "New Era"', *New Left Review* no. 237 (1999): 77–105.

Žižek, S. *Did Somebody Say Totalitarianism? Four Interventions in the (Mis) use of a Notion*, London, 2001.

INDEX